For a Wider World:

Sixty Works in the British Council Collection

KENT·INSTITUTE
OF·ART·&·DESIGN

Canterbury
New Dover Road
Canterbury
Kent
CT1 3AN

Tel: 01227 769371

Fax: 01227 817500

For a Wider World:

Sixty Works in the British Council Collection

The British Council

The British Council acknowledges the support of
Alltransport with the packing, transport and shipment
of these works for exhibition overseas.

Exhibition organised by: Andrea Rose,
Curator

Diana Eccles,
Assistant Curator

Biographies and
bibliographies
compiled by: James Bustard

Additional research: Emily Feaver

Photography: Rodney Todd-White
John Riddy

Catalogue designed by: Tim Harvey

Typeset by: The Printed Word Limited

Catalogue printed by: Lecturis bv. Eindhoven

ISBN: 0 86355 102 5

Quotations in the catalogue entries have been published
by kind permission of the following:

Yale University Press, London and New Haven
Barbican Art Gallery, London
Faber and Faber, London
Michael Russell, Salisbury
Royal Academy of Arts, London
Oxford University Press, Oxford
Tate Gallery, London; (Ben Nicholson literary
copyright)
Gordon Fraser, London
British Museum Publications, London
Lutterworth Press, Guildford and London
Arts Council of Great Britain
Whitworth Art Gallery, University of Manchester
Secker and Warburg, London
Thames and Hudson, London
Anthony d'Offay Gallery, London
Whitechapel Art Gallery, London
Ray Hughes Gallery, Queensland, Australia

cover illustration: Barry Flanagan. *The Cricketer* 1981 *(detail)*

FOREWORD

For over fifty years the British Council has been promoting cultural relations between Britain and other countries by providing access to British thought, experience, achievement and expertise. Much of what the Council does in the ninety countries where it is represented is intangible, involving the exchanges of people, the transfer of skills and the building of intellectual bridges – scientific, technological, academic, artistic, even personal.

One of the few areas of the Council's activities that is quite distinct is its collection of 20th century British art, known both nationally and internationally as the British Council Collection. This was first started in 1935, a year after the founding of the Council, and now numbers approximately 5,500 works. Here is solid, tangible, immediate evidence of a cultural activity that has grown up alongside the Council's more usual operations and forms a permanent, if different, aspect of its identity.

The Collection demonstrates the vitality of British art this century. It is used by museums and galleries both at home and abroad. A large part of it is on display throughout British Council offices and residences. But mostly it is used in the exhibitions that the British Council itself assembles.

These exhibitions seek to represent the achievements of British artists to audiences overseas, and it is a measure of their success that a large proportion of works in the Collection have either been donated by, or bought advantageously from, artists whose reputations abroad have been created and consolidated by the Council. Henry Moore, shown by the British Council at the 1948 Venice Biennale where he won the International Prize for Sculpture, is but one example among many of an artist who has endowed the Collection with his work, in recognition of the Council's role in bringing him to international prominence.

Sixty works out of a total of 5,500 cannot hope to tell the whole story. They can, I believe, reveal that the story of 20th century art in Britain is one of considerable richness, drama, even strangeness. From Sickert's painting of *St Mark's, Venice*, painted just over a hundred years ago, to Bill Woodrow's sculpture, *Point of Entry*, made last year for an exhibition at the Imperial War Museum, Britain's 'offshore' status – as an island so close to continental Europe and yet so individual in many respects – creates an underlying dynamic.

I hope these sixty works, representing some of the Council's most prized possessions, give an idea of some of the main themes and directions of the story of 20th century British art. Most importantly, I hope they show that it is a story worth listening to and that, like all good stories, it is one whose end you never really quite want to reach.

SIR RICHARD FRANCIS
Director General, The British Council

ACKNOWLEDGEMENTS

R H Alford

Julian Andrews

Lucy Aspinall

J A Barnett

Carol Beggs

Philip Blackman

Tom Buchanan

Ruth Bubb

Joan Burrows

James Bustard

Ruth Charity

Rita Charles

Graham Coe

Steve Court

Patrick Cunningham

Sandra Deighton

Neil Denman

Diana Eccles

David Evans

Mark Evans

Emily Feaver

William Feaver

Anneliese Greulich

John Hanson

Craig Henderson

Keith Hunter

Bert Kenny

Alice Keene

Catherine Kinley

John McGovern

Henry Meyric Hughes

Duncan Robinson

Terry Sandell

Dominic Scott

Brydon E Smith

David Thorp

Brian Vale

Michael Ward

Muriel Wilson

Paul Woodcock

Maggie Wyllie

Patsy Zeppel

INTRODUCTION

When Sickert went to Venice in 1896, he did the tourist sites like countless Englishmen before him. St. Mark's, the Salute, the Rialto, the Campanile and the Palazzo Ducale. Only Sickert wasn't quite English. 'Born in Munich in 1860, of pure Danish descent,' he used to boom across polite dinner-parties. 'No-one could be more English than I am'.

Sickert loved to rile. In London, he wore loud suits and cast around the music halls for his subjects ('deliberate vulgarity' said his critics). In Venice he was equally indelicate. The façade of St. Mark's, which he painted in several versions, is seen in the painting owned by the British Council spread right across the canvas. The ends are truncated. People pass in front like blurry photographs. The great weight of this 13th century structure, its vaults and chasms, domes and pinnacles, is presented as is. No gentle introduction or helpful presentational angle. Just the mass of stone and gold, head on.

St. Mark's was a fitting image to conclude the 19th and open the 20th century. Long the focus of Venice as a maritime empire, it had beckoned Englishmen across the seas to Europe throughout the 18th and 19th centuries. Ruskin, the greatest critic of the 19th century, saw it as the antithesis of all that was grim, dark and Protestant in England:

> '…there rises a vision out of the earth, and all the great square seems to have opened from it in a kind of awe, that one may see it far away… a treasure heap, it seems… beset with sculpture of alabaster… pillars of variegated stones… capitals rich with interwoven tracery… a confusion of delight…'
>
> (*Stones of Venice*, vol. II)

Turner too painted Venice as an effulgence. But the brilliance of Turner's Venetian pictures, with their radiant light so markedly in contrast with the half-tones and misty atmosphere of Britain, also masked a city declining in power and prestige. As Byron had written of Venice in *Childe Harold's Pilgrimage*:

> '…thy lot
> Is shameful to the nations – most of all
> Albion! to thee: the Ocean queen should not
> Abandon Ocean's children; in the fall
> Of Venice think of thine, despite thy watery wall.'
>
> (Canto VI, XVII)

so Turner saw Venice as a warning to Britain. She was at the height of her powers as a maritime empire, with naval supremacy ('Britannia rules the waves') and worldwide industrial expansion; but she too could be reduced to a tourist attraction, a glittering accumulation of past glories.

Britain's absorption of Sickert, as with so many artists of foreign extraction throughout the 20th century, was one way of keeping a native tendency to insularity at bay. With each absorption has come a readjustment, a realignment of our native contours. Sickert was a pupil of Whistler. Whistler himself was an American. His youth had been spent in Russia (where his father built the

Moscow – St. Petersburg railway), he had trained in Paris (where he knew Degas), and had finally settled in Britain, both as a refuge from America and as a good jumping-off point for the continent. Sickert originally signed his paintings 'Elève de Whistler', using French to emphasise the point that this was where modern art lay. His cosmopolitanism, his impatience with the introspection of British art at the time, impelled him to look across the Channel, first to France, then to Venice. And it was in Venice, alongside the remarkable paintings of St. Mark's, that he developed a series of nudes in interiors that were to have a profound effect on British painting in the 20th century.

Sickert offended propriety, but he stimulated British art into an immodesty that has all too rarely been attributed to the British character. Some artists didn't need much encouragement. Matthew Smith studied with Matisse in Paris some years before meeting Sickert, and his high-keyed Cornish landscapes of the 1920s and voluptuously handled nudes owe a debt both to Gauguin and Matisse. Gwen John studied under Whistler in Paris before 1900, and by 1904 had started to model for Rodin, for whom she nurtured a lifelong passion. Others, such as Spencer Gore and Harold Gilman, were encouraged to greater robustness by Sickert. Their views of Camden Town are Anglicisations of Impressionist vision: French clarity with an English ability to beef things up.

Twice this century, relations with the continent have been ruptured. During World War I, many of the artists who had done most to promote abstraction in Britain served on the Western Front. There, the crazed abstractions produced by the artillery and the devastation of all sense of order and rootedness, subdued much of their ardour for experimentation and subversion. Wadsworth, who had painted ships tricked out in dazzle-camouflage during the war (the industrial application of Vorticism), went to the Black Country in 1919 to paint the workings and slag heaps of the English midlands. His drawings still reverberate with the abstract patterning of the Western Front. But for the majority of artists, war reinforced their Englishness. William Roberts, a Vorticist before the war, tidied his figures into stolid, rhythmic patterns, a reminder of the Celtic qualities of interlacing and silhouette that have been important in British art for well over a thousand years. Burra revelled in the caustic and the narrative. David Jones, whose account of his experiences on the Western Front, *In Parenthesis*, is a memorable poetic narrative, delved back to the remote past, to the period when Britain belonged to the Roman Empire. Even a seemingly simple subject such as a view through a window is overlaid with the sense of times past, of innumerable spirits hovering in the air. In Jones too, the debt to Celtic art – the art of the Scots, the Welsh and the Irish – is vital.

One artist who needed no spur to 'Englishness' was Stanley Spencer. The British Council owns none of his great nude or figure paintings, but the three works shown here illustrate something of Spencer's conviction that Jerusalem could be built in England's green and pleasant land. Like William Blake, the 18th century poet, painter and revolutionary, Spencer's almost hallucinatory powers of description stem from reverence. When he describes not lying, but sitting like a bird on a groundsheet, not watching, but crawling like an ant up the stalk of a leaf, his peculiarly centrifugal vision is made palpable. Accusations of 'Englishness' (like some sort of anti-social disease) have often been laid on him, but Spencer was a radical in the most fundamental sense. Like Constable a century before, the intensity of his attachment to a particular locale carried him ever deeper into it. For Constable it was the landscape of the River Stour near Dedham in Suffolk. For Spencer it was the village of Cookham on the River Thames. In both cases the urgency led to possession, and it is this rootedness, this exclusivity, that has sometimes seemed an impediment to wider appreciation. Spencer, like Constable before him, lies at one extreme of a notion of 'Englishness'. (The other extreme in Constable's case being Turner, an artist of breathtaking range and a ceaseless European traveller.) Yet within the province that he claimed as his own, he dug deeper, and more adventurously, than anyone before him. It is to his credit that he has taken 'Englishness' to include some of the most direct and outspoken images this century.

Curiously, for a nation still in possession of an empire, few artists who looked outside Britain before World War II looked further than Europe. (It had to wait until after the empire was gone for artists such Howard Hodgkin to discover India, Richard Long Africa, Michael Andrews Australia.) Henry Moore was an exception. The African and Pre-Columbian sculpture that he saw in the British Museum in the 1920s inspired his wholly new interpretation of the body. Moore's re-forming of the classical figure belongs not so much to the English, but to the European mainstream – Picasso, Cézanne, Rodin, Brancusi – but it also owes something to the physical background of England, the great shoulders of land that rise from the sea, the softly undulating downland, the wealds, standing stones and fossilised compressions of rock that make up the ancient countryside. Paul Nash, too, was inspired by an ancient Britain. The prehistoric sites around Stonehenge, where megaliths and grave-mounds still lie, invoked for him a powerful 'sense of place', as they have done far more recently in the work of Richard Long, whose stone lines and circles conjure up a sense of druidic awe.

The surrealism implicit in Nash's landscapes – the poetic possibilities of presenting odd combinations of objects – was given added meaning by the outbreak of World War II. As during the First War, though this time on a more organised footing, the Ministry of Information set up a War Artists Advisory Committee to recruit artists to make a pictorial record of all aspects of war, both military and civilian. Ravilious was set to work making watercolours of coastal defences. The weird installations and patterned convoys processing off into the sky (actually on their way to Russia) in Ravilious' watercolour are echoed in the work of John Tunnard. The Kafkaesque helplessness of war is demonstrated in Tunnard by his abandonment of all known configurations of reality. The abstract images that he invented make passing reference to radar and gale warnings, but also signal an inability to face up to reality for one minute longer.

Once more, war encouraged 'Englishness'. Conscious of being a small island on the defensive, for some years almost alone in fighting the forces of Fascism, British artists retreated within the 'watery wall', developing a tight and wiry style, known as 'Neo-Romanticism', that dramatised the landscape. Graham Sutherland was one of its chief exponents. Even after the war, his interest in the thorn as a symbol of cruelty (as also with Lucian Freud, in his painting of a girl grasping a thorn-stemmed rose of 1948) is presented with a concentration and hysterical stillness that come close to mania.

Relief came in the shape of America. The St. Ives' group of painters, among them Peter Lanyon and Roger Hilton, coincided with the rising star of American Abstract Expressionism at the end of the 40s. With Europe exhausted, Britain turned its westernmost face towards the Atlantic, where limits seemed non-existent. Jackson Pollock in New York was flinging paint onto canvas, making the act of painting into some sort of entranced performance. Clyfford Still seemed able to drown his primordial landscapes in sheer torrential power. Their pictorial muscle was invigorating, but it was the cue in Britain not so much for violent gesture as for lyrical personal expression. 'Painting is a bird on the wing', said Ben Nicholson, most influential of the artists who had settled in St. Ives before the war. In this westernmost outpost of Britain, 400 miles from London, he, his wife the sculptor, Barbara Hepworth, and Naum Gabo, the Russian constructivist who had settled in Britain in 1936, had kept alive the possibilities for abstract art, seeing it as a key to universal harmonies, a clarification of essentials. Peter Lanyon seized the opportunity. Keeping close to the land – unlike his American counterparts – he pushed and pulled it into shape, upending rocks, stockpiling landmarks, unleashing himself upon the landscape like a force of nature himself. The nice art of topography (the careful delineation of land and estate) was shattered.

After the war, many other assumptions were also shattered. Britain no longer had an empire (one is reminded of it today only in a faraway venture like the Falklands War (1982), commemorated so unheroically in Bill Woodrow's *Point of Entry*). Its wealth was considerably diminished. And its position on the world stage was now marginal, not central. It was natural to turn to America.

America had officially declared history 'bunk' (Henry Ford). America was affluent. American roots lay in an economic democracy, not the bankrupt class systems of Europe. And most of all, America spoke English (no need to write 'Elève de Whistler' at the bottom of the canvas any more).

Expansiveness followed. Anthony Caro, who first visited the States in 1959, was fired by a nation unencumbered by long traditions of funerary, votive or commemorative statuary. He discovered the freedom to get sculpture off its plinth and onto the floor. He discovered that sculpture could have reach; that it needn't disguise its origins; that it could approximate to landscape, if it wanted to, like big, abstract, American painting. Edouardo Paolozzi welcomed the eclecticism of America. David Hockney found its vulgarity salutary, as Sickert had discovered vulgarity to be half a century earlier. Richard Smith discovered that rules existed to be broken, that if sculpture could approximate to paintings, then paintings could approximate to sculpture. He took the stretchers from his canvas, releasing the picture plane from its centuries-old rigidity, and let it all hang loose.

Expansiveness was followed by a period of experimentation, of taking nothing on trust. Two of the most intrepid explorers were Bridget Riley and Richard Long, who, in quite different ways, discarded conventional notions of landscape – one of the most deep-rooted of all English sensibilities – to recast it in hitherto unknown forms. Bridget Riley's seething and engulfing canvases, which express the dynamism of nature rather than the appearance of tree stumps and wooded glades, have strong echoes of the vortices and burning suns in the paintings of JMW Turner; those huge cosmic forces that dissolve and nullify all matter until it resembles only light, colour, air. The fields of energy that she creates, with their sources of stability and instability constantly within vision, are perhaps closer to classical painting than any other produced in Britain this century; their relentless formalism never quite reduces the sense of impending doom.

Richard Long is not interested in tree stumps and wooded glades either, or rather he is, but in relation to the time it takes him to walk past them. His is an art of association. The text panels that he produces as a result of walking through an area have the power of poetry to resonate by striking deep chords of reference and memory. The language that he uses is plain, consonant, keeping as close to Saxon and Celtic roots as it can, like an axe on stone. Words follow place: Liskeard, Bodmin, Porlock, drawing out as he passes them the image of the geological formation beneath them (granite), the earthworks upon them, the atmosphere about them, the language that has formed them and which in turn is now informing us. As he walks the tumuli and burial mounds of this ancient part of Cornwall the circles he describes are felicitously re-enacted in the very word 'moor', with its double circles in the centre. His unadorned language, and the simplicity of his method – 23 bars of Cornish slate on the floor as *Stone Line* – keep control of a submerged lyricism. Like Wordsworth in the Lucy poems an animist feeling for the earth is set out in the most elemental forms:

> 'No motion has she now, no force;
> She neither hears nor sees;
> Rolled round in earth's diurnal course
> With rocks, and stones, and trees.'

> *A Slumber did my spirit seal.*

It would be forcing the argument to describe Long and Riley as heirs to Constable and Turner. Their innovation however is basically of a European tradition of seeing, a tradition which British artists have increasingly turned to again over the last two decades. Even at the height of the 'Pop' art movement in the early 60s, when his peers were looking towards America, Patrick Caulfield was re-examining the worn-out conventions of European painting – the still-life, the interior, the 'view'. In his recent work, *The Blue Posts*, the pub interior becomes the arena in which central concerns in European paintings are addressed: the way light falls, how to organise a space, the reconciliation of different ways of looking at things (the wedge of pink-stripe wallpaper, the photo-realistic half-pint of lager, the overall baize-green ambience of the place).

Taking the big European themes and having them out in the local. This could almost be the theme for the most fertile developments in British art in recent years, both in sculpture and painting. A younger generation of sculptors, among them Tony Cragg, Bill Woodrow and Richard Deacon, has discovered its own backyard. Being Londoners, that means a rising tide of jettisoned car parts, dated lino flooring and moulded plastics. In their hands, these poor, unlovely materials are transformed into what Tony Cragg has described as 'the new nature', objects that can be set alongside the images of the naturally occurring world so that 'when the tigers die out, as the dragons did, there will be something equivalent to take their place'.

For an older generation of Londoners too, European art has been at the heart of a revolution. The group of artists loosely associated as the 'School of London' – among them Francis Bacon, Lucian Freud, Frank Auerbach, Leon Kossoff and R. B. Kitaj – has concentrated almost exclusively on figure painting and places they know well. Like Sickert, many of them were not born in Britain. Like Sickert, they have brought urgency and compulsion to British art. Francis Bacon, sadly not represented in the British Council Collection, was the first to demonstrate, in the late 1940s, that the figure could be prime material for painting once more, even if it was only a blind, dismembered figure howling with rage and pain. Those associated with him have not flinched. Their job of resuscitating a tradition thought to have been finally killed off in World War II has involved some of the most gruelling and penetrating acts of observation this century. The fact that they have produced works as remarkable as Lucian Freud's *Naked girl with egg* and Frank Auerbach's *Head of JYM III* underlines that British art has not succumbed to the condition of a 'treasure heap', but that it has gone well beyond.

ANDREA ROSE
Curator, The British Council Collection

THE CATALOGUE

Dimensions are given in centimetres. Height precedes width.
Dimensions are of the original surface, without mount or frame.

Inscriptions are noted with abbreviations to indicate their position
eg. brc – bottom right corner.

All quotations under individual entries are by the artist,
unless stated otherwise.

I

Walter Richard Sickert 1860 – 1942
St Mark's, Venice c. 1896 – 7

oil on canvas
100.3 × 151.1
inscribed brc. Sickert
given by Mrs B D'Oyly Carte, March 1951

'We are fond in England of talking of 'refinement' and by refinement we do not at all mean what the French mean when they say 'raffinement'. The word 'refinement' as currently used in England stands, I believe, for a highly-cultivated capacity for suffering acutely from noise, from the smell of inferior tobacco, from inferior clothes, from inferior cooking… With this goes, in the region of taste, an utter impossibility of living for twenty-four hours in a room with a *wrong* wallpaper, and as a corollary of the wallpaper, a mild liking for inoffensive and slight watercolours in the *right* mounts, and framed the *right* way. For guidance in these matters we rely entirely on *snobisme*… The refined are perhaps further from art, which is a robust and racy wench than any other class.'

The New Age 28 July 1910

'Taste is the death of a painter… The more our art is serious, the more it will tend to avoid the drawing-room and stick to the kitchen. The plastic arts are gross arts, dealing joyously with gross material facts. They call, in their servants, for a robust stomach and a great power of endurance, and while they will flourish in the scullery, or on the dunghill, they fade at a breath from the drawing-room.'

The Art News 12 May 1910

2

GWEN JOHN

Head of a Woman (Chloe Boughton Leigh?) c. 1910

pencil and wash on paper

16.5 × 17

inscribed blc: Gwen John

purchased October 1948

'I want my drawings if they are drawings to be definite and clean like Japanese drawings. But I have not succeeded yet. I think even if I don't do a good one the work of deciding on the exact tones and colour and seeing so many 'pictures' – as one sees each drawing as a picture – and the practice of putting things down with decision ought to help me when I do a painting in oils – in fact I think all is there – except the modelling of flesh perhaps.'

Letter of 15 February 1909 from Gwen John to Ursula Tyrwhitt, published in *Gwen John* by Cecily Langdale, Yale University Press, 1987

3

SPENCER GORE 1878 – 1914
Mornington Crescent c. 1911

oil on canvas
50.8 × 61.6
purchased March 1948

'I always find things interesting as they are, or, if you like, interesting because they are so. I am perfectly incapable of inventing the shape of a stone or how it lies on the top of another or how it would be related to everything else.'

Spencer Gore, The Minories, Colchester, 1970

'There was a few months ago a month of June which Gore verily seems to have used as if he had known that it was to be for him the last of its particularly fresh and sumptuous kind. He used it to look down on the garden of Mornington Crescent. The trained trees rise and droop in fringes, like fountains, over the little well of greenness and shade where parties of young people are playing at tennis. The backcloth is formed by the tops of the brown houses of the Hampstead Road and the liver-coloured titles of the Tube Station.'

W R Sickert in an obituary tribute to Spencer Gore, *The New Age* 9 April 1914

4

HAROLD GILMAN 1876 – 1919
Shopping List c. 1912

oil on canvas
61.5 × 31
inscribed brc: H Gilman
purchased March 1948

'Life dictates the shapes, the artist only holds them. If forms don't please, look for another motive. Nothing but life can imitate the real.'

The Art News 25 May 1910

'There was a parsonic honesty in his painting; a moral rectitude in his pursuit of pictorial truth … he had every virtue of middle-class England.'

Wyndham Lewis in an obituary note on Gilman in *Harold Gilman; An Appreciation* by Wyndham Lewis, Chatto and Windus, 1919

5

MATTHEW SMITH 1879 – 1959
Fitzroy Street Nude No. 2 1916

oil on canvas
101.5 × 76
inscribed br: MS
purchased March 1948

'I long for Rutter[†] to be told that my representation of women is sane, and healthy, a state usually unattractive to "refined" taste. I admit, also, that they are derived from Rubens and Delacroix, with an eye on Courbet, Ingres and perhaps Renoir, and not the prostitutes of Rouault.'

[†]Frank Rutter, (1876 – 1937) Art Critic and Writer, founding editor of *The Art News*

'Extract from a biographical study' by Mary Keene, *Matthew Smith,* Barbican Art Gallery, 1983

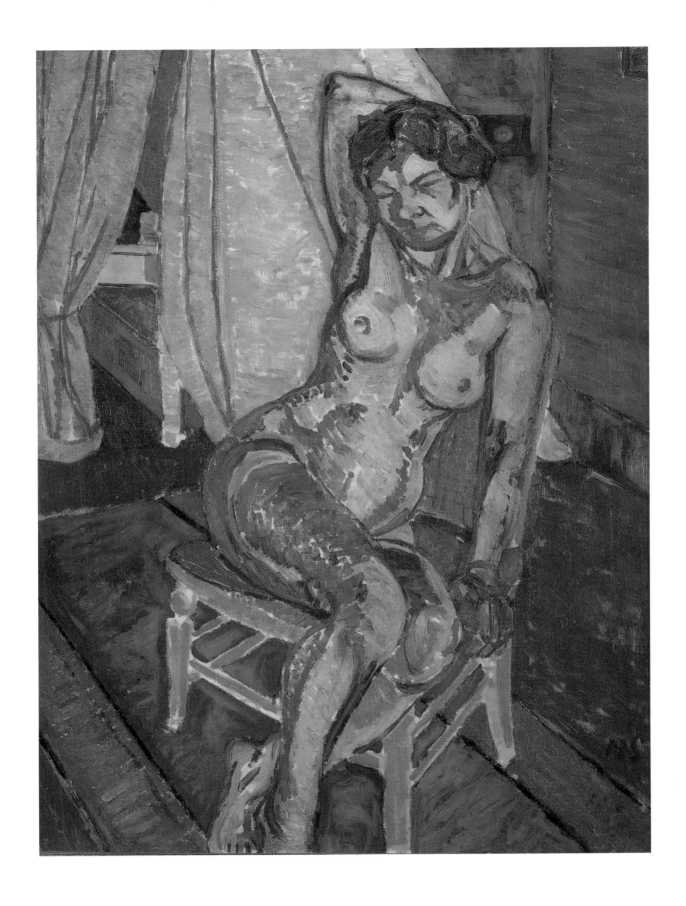

6

STANLEY SPENCER 1891 – 1959
Soldiers at Thanksgiving Service 1918 – 1919

wash on paper – squared up for enlargement

54 × 53·5

purchased 1948

'My first outdoor anchorage seemed to be the Church. Somehow religion was something to do with me, and I was to do with religion. It came into my vision quite naturally like the sky and rain… My early work was, as far as specified religion is concerned, non-denominational, but whatever was the direction, it was utterly believed in. It is just that, as I said, it was nevertheless in harmony with known Christian religion and ideals means that whatever I love and have to do nowadays, if it is not in harmony with Christianity then I am still faithfully trying to turn and keep in the Christian direction… I don't keep to the rules… I dislike many of them and think them harmful to what I love and hope for in humanity. Nevertheless, these things, as I said, are an essential part of the Christian qualities.'

Stanley Spencer at War by Richard Carline, Faber and Faber, 1978

7

EDWARD WADSWORTH 1889 – 1949

Ladle Slag 1919

ink and watercolour on paper

35 × 40

inscribed brc. Edward Wadsworth 1919

purchased August 1950

From Wyndham Lewis' recollections of Wadsworth after his death, first published in *The Listener*, describing a car trip in the North of England 1920:

'Wadsworth taking me in his car on a tour of some Yorkshire's cities. In due course we arrived on a hill above Halifax. He stopped and gazed down into its blackened labyrinth. I could see that he was proud of it. "It's beautiful. It's just like Hell, isn't it?", he said enthusiastically.'

Edward Wadsworth: A Painter's Life by Barbara Wadsworth, Michael Russell, 1989

8

MATTHEW SMITH 1879 – 1959
A Winding Road – Cornish Landscape 1920

oil on canvas

53.5 × 65

purchased March 1948

painted during the wet summer of 1920, at St Columb Major, Cornwall

'They all praise the colour, but if the pictures hold together, there must be something else, you know, there must be something else… Feeling is all very well, but there must be science too.'

Matthew Smith, Royal Academy of Arts, 1960

9

Henry Moore 1898 – 1988
Girl with Clasped Hands 1930

Cumberland alabaster
38.1 high
purchased March 1948

'I am very much aware that associational, psychological factors play a large part in sculpture. The meaning and significance of form itself probably depends on the countless associations of man's history. For example, rounded forms convey an idea of fruitfulness, maturity, probably because the earth, women's breasts, and most fruits are rounded, and these shapes are important because they have this background in our habits of perception. I think the humanist organic element will always be for me of fundamental importance in sculpture, giving sculpture its vitality. Each particular carving I make takes on in my mind a human, or occasionally animal character and personality, and this personality controls its design and formal qualities, and makes me satisfied or dissatisfied with the work as it develops.'

'The Sculptor Speaks', *The Listener*, 18 August 1937

BEN NICHOLSON 1894 – 1982
Still Life (Greek Landscape) 1931 – 1936

oil and pencil on canvas
68.5 × 77.5
purchased July 1948

'One of the main differences between a representational and an abstract painting is that the former can transport you to Greece by a representation of blue skies and seas, olive trees and marble columns, but in order that you may take part in this you will have to concentrate on the painting, whereas the abstract version by its free use of form and colour will be able to give you the actual quality of Greece itself, and this will become a part of the light and space and life in the room – there is no need to concentrate, *it becomes* a part of living.'

'Notes on "Abstract" Art' October 1941, revised 1948 in *Ben Nicholson: A Studio International Special* ed. Maurice de Sausmarez *Studio International,* 1969

II

David Jones
Curtained Outlook 1932

pencil and watercolour on paper
78.5 × 55
purchased May 1949

'I always work from the window of a house if it is at all possible. I like looking out on the world from a reasonably sheltered position. I can't paint in the wind, and I like the indoors–outdoors, contained yet limitless feeling of windows and doors. A man should be in a house; a beast should be in a field, and all that. The rambling, familiar, south, walled, small, flower-beddedness of Pigotts[†] and the space, park, north, serene, clear silverness of Rock[††] in Northumberland both did something.'

[†]Pigotts Farm, Buckinghamshire, home of Eric Gill and family
[††] Rock Hall, home of Helen Sutherland, noted patron of the arts

Notes made at Jim Ede's request for the Tate Gallery in 1935. Text published in *David Jones*, Tate Gallery, 1981

12

Henry Moore 1898 – 1988
Composition 1933

carved concrete
58.4 high
purchased March 1948

'The Africans never worked in outline, they always looked into the middle of their subject, taking out the parts they wanted to depress and leaving the parts they wanted to project. After watching African carvers at the 1924 Wembley exhibition I decided that it was their use of the adze, rather than an axe, that enabled them to work in this way, and I designed one to use myself.'

Henry Moore at the British Museum, British Museum, 1981

'The sculpture which moves me most is full-blooded and self-supporting, fully in the round, that is, its component forms are completely realized and work as masses in opposition, not being merely indicated by surface cutting in relief; it is not perfectly symmetrical, it is static and it is strong and vital, giving out something of the power of great mountains. It has a life of its own, independent of the object it represents.'

'A View of Sculpture', *The Architectural Association Journal,* May 1930

13

PAUL NASH 1889 – 1946
Landscape of the Megaliths 1934

oil on canvas
49.5 × 73
inscribed blc: Paul Nash
purchased July 1946

'Last summer, I walked in a field near Avebury where two rough monoliths stood up sixteen feet high, miraculously patterned with black and orange lichen, remnants of the avenue of stones that leads to the Great Circle. A mile away, a green pyramid casts its gigantic shadow. In the hedge, at hand, the white trumpet of a convulvulus turns from its spiral stem, following the sun. In my art I would solve such an equation.'

Unit One ed. Herbert Read, Cassell, 1934

'I've read somewhere that certain primitive peoples coming across a large block of stone in their wanderings would worship it as a God – which is easy to understand, for there is a sense of immense power about a large rough-shaped lump of rock or stone.'

Henry Moore in a letter to Nash, 1933, after seeing Avebury: 15 September, 1933, quoted in *Paul Nash* by Andrew Causey, Clarendon Press, 1980

EDWARD BURRA 1905 – 1976
The Band 1934

watercolour on paper
55.5 × 76
inscribed bl: Burrito 34
purchased August 1950

'Really dearie if only you all were here New Y is marvellous. Am comfortably ensconsed in Harlem 1890 7 Av (apartment 2A) in a pitch dark bedroom of a pitch dark apartment the property of Edna and Lloyd Thomas who are both charming… We went to a little party the other night to a hermeticaly sealed "oriental" flat lit by old moorish incence burners with red electric bulbs you couldnt see a thing theres so much talent at the partys here that its more like non stop variety we went to an outrageous place called the theatrical grill a cellar done up to look like Napoleans tomb and lit in such a way that all the white people look like corpses. Ive never seen such faces the best gangster pictures are far outdone by the old original thing.

'The chief attractes of the cabaret was "Gloria Swanson" a mountainous coal black nigger in a crepe de chine dress trimmed sequins who rushed about screaming Clappy weather, just cant keep my old arse together keeps runnin all the time etc and rush up to the table dragging his sequins up and disclosing a filthy dirty pair of pink silk panties how he managed I dont know no balls or anything else as far as I could see…'

Letter to William Chappell from 1890 7th Avenue Apt. 2A NYC, 18 October 1933 (no punctuation) in *Well Dearie! The Letters of Edward Burra* ed. William Chappell, Gordon Fraser, 1985

15

BEN NICHOLSON 1894 – 1982
White Relief 1935

oil on canvas and built-up wood

54.5 × 80

purchased March 1948

'I don't call the "carved reliefs" "coloured" because this conjures up an idea of a "surface colouring" whereas the colour of stone or wood or I hope these reliefs runs right through the material and comes out on the other side.'

Letter to Ronald Alley, 14 August 1962, published in *Ben Nicholson,* Tate Gallery, 1969, p6

'I find I judge paintings by the quality of light given off…in my own work it is my only way of judging its achievement or progress.'

Architectural Review, October 1935 (Paul Nash quoting Ben Nicholson in a review of the exhibition of carved reliefs)

16
HENRY MOORE 1898 – 1988
Mother and Child 1936

Ancaster stone
51 high
purchased March 1948

'Abstract qualities of design are essential to the value of a work, but to me of equal importance is the psychological, human element. If both abstract and human elements are welded together in a work, it must have a fuller, deeper meaning.'

'The Sculptor's Aims', *Unit One,* ed. Herbert Read, Cassell, 1934

'From very early on I have had an obsession with the "Mother and Child" theme. It has been a universal theme from the beginning of time and some of the earliest sculptures we've found from the Neolithic Age are of a mother and child.'

Henry Moore: My Ideas, Inspiration and Life as an Artist by Henry Moore and John Hedgecoe, Ebury Press, 1986

17

WILLIAM ROBERTS 1895 – 1980
Folk Dance 1938

watercolour on paper – squared up for enlargement
21.5 × 32
purchased July 1942

'Several years ago there was an advertisement that appeared in the newspapers that impressed me very much; it showed a man bending forward and clutching his back with one hand in a sudden gesture of agony; beneath the design were the words: "Every picture tells a story". Pictures, of course, have always told stories; the cave-man's scenes of hunting: Greek art illustrating the legends of Gods and Heroes; and the works of the medieval painters, relating the doings of soldiers and saints. However, in more recent times, a theory has been expounded, which states that a picture should not tell a story. It was after Cézanne, with the début of Picasso, and the rise of Cubism that certain art chroniclers and critics began to hold forth against the picture with a story. Roger Fry and Clive Bell were especially critical of the story-telling painting. For them the important quality in a picture was its "Significant Form", its "significant combinations of significant form', and "Form is the Talisman". This line has been followed through all the "Isms" of modern painting; until with the Actionists, Tachists, and the latest "Contemporaries", even "Significant Form" can be discarded"; for all that matters now is "Significant Paint"… the canvas becomes empty of all subject matter, except the dabs, smudges, and trickles of the paint itself…'

'Comments'. *Paintings, Drawings,* Canale Publications, 1964

18

HENRY MOORE 1898 – 1988
Brown Tube Shelter 1940

ink, wash and crayon on paper
54.5 × 32
inscribed brc: Moore 40
given by the War Artists' Advisory Committee, November 1949

'I was fascinated by the sight of people camping out deep under the ground. I had never seen so many rows of reclining figures and even the holes out of which the trains were coming seemed to me to be like the holes in my sculpture. And there were intimate little touches. Children fast sleep, with trains roaring past only a couple of yards away. People who were obviously strangers to one another forming tight little intimate groups. They were cut off from what was happening above, but they were aware of it. There was a tension in the air. They were a bit like the chorus in a Greek drama telling us about the violence we don't actually witness.'

Henry Moore: *A Shelter Sketchbook,* British Museum Publications, 1988

19

ERIC RAVILIOUS 1903 – 1942
Convoy passing an island 1940 – 41

watercolour on paper
49.5 × 54
inscribed brc: Eric Ravilious
given by the War Artists' Advisory Committee, June 1946

'I've landed here by way of a destroyer – and an RAF launch – and am now living with this small naval mess, five officers and a few ratings. They are all very nice people. The island is rocky and rolling and wild, in peacetime a bird sanctuary. Hoodie crows and golden-crested wrens are about; I wish you could see the island. You would love it. There is the oldest beacon – 1636 – in the centre (you light a fire on the roof of a thing like a large dovecot) and the turf is just like a pile carpet. They took me to the lighthouse lantern this morning. I've just been entranced with the place all day and explored without working so must have an early bed (one game of darts) and work early tomorrow.'

From RN Signal Station, May Island, to his wife Tirzah, October 1940, published in *Eric Ravilious: Memoir of an Artist* by Helen Binyon, Lutterworth Press, 1983

20

HENRY MOORE 1898 – 1988
Row of Sleepers 1941

watercolour and ink on paper
54·5 × 32
inscribed brc: Moore 1941
given by the War Artists' Advisory Committee, November 1949

'There'd been air-raids in the other war, but the only thing at all like those shelters that I could think of was the hold of a slave-ship on its way from Africa to America, full of hundreds of people who were having things done to them that they were quite powerless to resist.'

Henry Moore on Sculpture, MacDonald and Co, 1966

21

JOHN TUNNARD 1900 – 1971
The Trial 1944

watercolour and gouache on paper
37.2 × 55.2
inscribed blc: John Tunnard '44 D116
purchased July 1948

'I started certainly as a representational painter and moved through various phases of representationalism. First, I suppose, I was interested in merely trying to put down what I saw or thought I saw. Then, after that, I was more interested in the dramatic contour of the landscape or whatever it was that I was painting, and then, more particularly, not so much with the literary dramatic content but with the geometrically dramatic content. By that I mean the dramatic movement of roads, of rats sweeping into the farmyard, of the lines of telegraph poles or the sweeps of railings, and there I found myself exaggerating to get the geometrically dramatic. Of course, I got to the stage when, confronted with a landscape, I felt that I could not be bound by the things that I saw, and naturally the only thing to do was to invent. As soon as I started inventing I found that it was so much more exciting, and that inventing came gradually into what is called non-representational painting.'

Interview with Myerscough Walker, April 1944, in *John Tunnard,* Arts Council of Great Britain, 1977

22

Graham Sutherland 1903 – 1980
Landscape with Estuary 1945

gouache and chalk on paper

41 × 68

purchased August 1950

painted at the estuary in South Pembrokeshire called Sandy Haven

'It was in 1934 that I first visited Pembrokeshire. After a good deal of wandering about I came upon two very remarkable passages of country situated in the arms of land which embrace the great area of St Bride's Bay. The southern slopes yield to the plain…here the land, gradually sloping to the sea, is studded with cairns of every size. Between these are fields, each with a spear of rock at its centre. It is as if the solid rock foundation of the earth had thrown up these spears to transfix and hold the scanty earth of the fields upon it. Farms and cottages – glistening white, pink and blue-grey – give scale and quicken by their implications our apprehensions of the scene… In this direction, nearer the sea, the earth is comparatively flat, but this flatness is deceiving and makes the discovery of little steep valleys more surprising. These valleys possess a bud-like intricacy of form and contain streams, often of indescribable beauty, which run to the sea. To see a solitary human figure descending upon such a road at the solemn moment of the sunset is to realise that enveloping quality of the earth, which can create, as it does here, a mysterious space limit, a womb-like enclosure, which gives the human form an extraordinary force and significance.'

Letter to Colin Anderson, published in *Horizon,* April 1942

23

PAUL NASH 1889 – 1946
Eclipse of the Sunflower 1945

oil on canvas
71.1 × 91.4
incscibed blc: Paul Nash
purchased May 1949

'In the Solstice the spent sun shines from its zenith encouraging the Sunflower in the dual role of sun and firewheel to perform its mythological purpose. The sun appears to be whipping the Sunflower like a top. The Sunflower Wheel tears over the hill cutting a path through the standing corn and bounding into the air as it gathers momentum. This is the blessing of The Midsummer Fire.'

From *Picture History* (a series of texts on his paintings produced by Nash for his dealer, Dudley Tooth), 1945. Quoted in *Paul Nash* by Andrew Causey, Clarendon Press, 1980

24

STANLEY SPENCER 1891 – 1959
Bluebells, Cornflowers and Rhododendrum 1945

oil on canvas
50.8 × 76.2
purchased June 1950

'There are two parts of myself, one is me, and the other is the life around me that is me also. I am aware that all sorts of parts of me are lying about waiting to join me. It is the way I complete and fulfill myself.'

'Stanley Spencer and the art of his time' by Andrew Causey, *Stanley Spencer,* Royal Academy of Arts, 1980

25

GRAHAM SUTHERLAND 1903 – 1980
Thorn Tree 1945 – 6

oil on canvas
127 × 101.5
inscribed brc: Sutherland
purchased November 1948

'My thorn trees came into being in a curious way. I had been asked (in February 1944) by the Vicar of St Matthews, Northampton, to paint a Crucifixion. In the autumn of that year I had been thinking of the form the work was to take; in the spring of the following year the subject was still very much in my mind. So far I had made no drawings, and I went into the country. For the first time I started to notice thorn bushes, and the structure of thorns as they pierced the air. I made some drawings, and as I made them, a curious change developed. As the thorns rearranged themselves, they became, whilst still retaining their own pricking, space-encompassing life, something else – a kind of "stand-in" for a Crucifixion and a crucified head. The thorns sprang from the idea of potential cruelty – and to me they *were* the cruelty; and I attempted to give the idea a double twist, as it were, by setting them in benign circumstances: blue skies, green grass, Crucifixions under warmth…'

'Thoughts on Painting', *The Listener,* September 1951

26

BEN NICHOLSON 1894 – 1982
Mousehole November 11 1947 1947

oil on canvas mounted on wood
46.5 × 58.5
purchased November 1948

'My "still-life" paintings are closely identified with landscape, more closely than are my landscapes which relate perhaps more to still-life.'

Statements: A Review of British Abstract Art in 1956, Institute of Contemporary Arts, 1957

'In painting a "still-life" one takes the simple every-day-forms of a bottle-mug-jug-plate-on-table as the basis for the expression of an idea; the forms are not entirely free though they are free to the extent that each object can be seen from as many viewpoints as you wish at one and the same time but the colours are free: bottle colour for plate, plate colour for table, or just as you wish and working in this way you have in time not a still-life or objects but an equivalent of something much more like deer passing through a winter forest, over foothills and mountains, through sunlight and shadows in Arizona, Cornwall or Provence and so, inevitably, you eventually at some point discard altogether the forms of even the simplest objects as a basis and work out your idea, not only in free colour but also in free form.'

Ben Nicholson: A Studio International Special ed. Maurice de Sausmarez, Studio International, 1969

27

STANLEY SPENCER 1891 – 1959
Port Glasgow Cemetery 1947

oil on canvas

50.8 × 76.2

purchased August 1948

a view of the cemetery at Port Glasgow which Spencer discovered while

working as an official war artist at the nearby Lithgows Shipyards

during World War II

'One evening in Port Glasgow, when unable to write due to a jazz band playing in the drawing-room just below me, I walked up along the road past the gas works to where I saw a cemetery on a gently rising slope… I seemed then to see that it rose in the midst of a great plain and that all in the plain were resurrecting and moving towards it… I knew then that the resurrection would be directed from that hill.'

Stanley Spencer: Resurrection Pictures 1945 – 50, by R. H. Wilenski, Faber, 1951

28

LUCIAN FREUD b. 1922
Girl with roses 1947 – 48

oil on canvas
106 × 75
purchased December 1948

'A painter must think of everything he sees as being there entirely for his own use and pleasure. The artist who tries to serve nature is only an executive artist. And, since the model he so painfully copies is not going to be hung up next to the picture, since the picture is going to be there on its own, it is of no interest whether it is an accurate copy of the model. Whether it will convince or not, depends entirely on what it is in itself, what is there to be seen. The model should only serve the very private function for the painter of providing the starting point for his excitement. The effect in space of two different human individuals can be as different as the effect of a candle and an electric light bulb. Therefore the painter must be concerned with the air surrounding his subject as with that subject itself. It is through observation and perception of atmosphere that he can register the feeling that he wishes his painting to give out.'

'Some thoughts on painting', *Encounter*, vol. 3. July 1954

29

PETER LANYON 1918 – 1964

Bojewyan Farms 1951 – 52

oil on masonite

121.9 × 243.9

inscribed brc: Peter Lanyon '52

purchased December 1961

'Bojewyan is a small village near St Just, probably one of the most ancient and primitive parts of the district. This is not a mining but a farming picture – a bucolic scene, rather earthy. It's also a triptych with three sections to it. On the left there is the sea at the top, and the grass and hayricks. The middle is some sort of animal, even a hand, and on the right is the chaff which comes from corn and harvesting. In some ways it is a picture about birth and life and death, which is why it belongs with the Crucifixion triptych. Dry stone walls that run round the fields in this part of Cornwall divide up the sections of Bojewyan Farms.'

From a recorded talk, 1963, published in *Peter Lanyon*, Whitworth Art Gallery, 1978

30

ROGER HILTON 1911 – 1975
October '56 (Brown, Black and White) 1956

oil on canvas
140 × 127
purchased July 1962

'Abstraction in itself is nothing. It is only a step towards a new sort of figuration, that is, one which is more true. However beautiful they may be, one can no longer depict women as Titian did. Renoir in his last pictures had already greatly modified her shape. Today one sees people who are changing abstraction into landscape (the easiest to do). For an abstract painter there are two ways out or on: he must give up painting and take to architecture, or he must reinvent figuration.

Now that we have conquered new plastic ground during the last fifty years, there is no reason why images should not return without fear of repeating what has already been done.'

Roger Hilton, Galerie Charles Leinhard, Zurich, 1961

31

EDUARDO PAOLOZZI b. 1924

Collage 1956

mixed media and collage on paper

38 × 47

purchased December 1959

'For the young artist wandering round a large city like London he will find a super abundance of raw materials…any amount of various woods, papers, ropes, beds, parts of kitchens, plastic bags full of danger, textiles, enough magazines to make six thousand collages.'

Lost Magic Kingdoms, 1985

32

EDUARDO PAOLOZZI b. 1924
Mask 1957

watercolour and collage on paper
68.5 × 50
inscribed brc: Eduardo Paolozzi 1957
purchased December 1959

'Reality surpasses the fictions of even the wildest imagination. Like a machine for milking a rat. Incredible, yet it actually exists.... The public's dilemma comes from the fact that they're still looking for objects, you see, objects in the fine-art tradition, and it's this kind of object the public usually gets.... I like to think that the Olivetti things[†] take a cool look at a special kind of pornography, the pornography of human values. And in a way, forcing people to look at a state they accept, like having monkeys working with computers, and also perhaps suggesting the kind of corporate image, the faceless man...the faceless white-collar worker turning into a mechanical man. It's not just technology, it's looking with as fresh an eye as possible at the whole realm of human experience.'

[†]a series of etchings made for British Olivetti Ltd.

From 'Speculative Illustrations' Paolozzi in conversation with J G Ballard and Frank Whitford, *Studio International,* October 1971

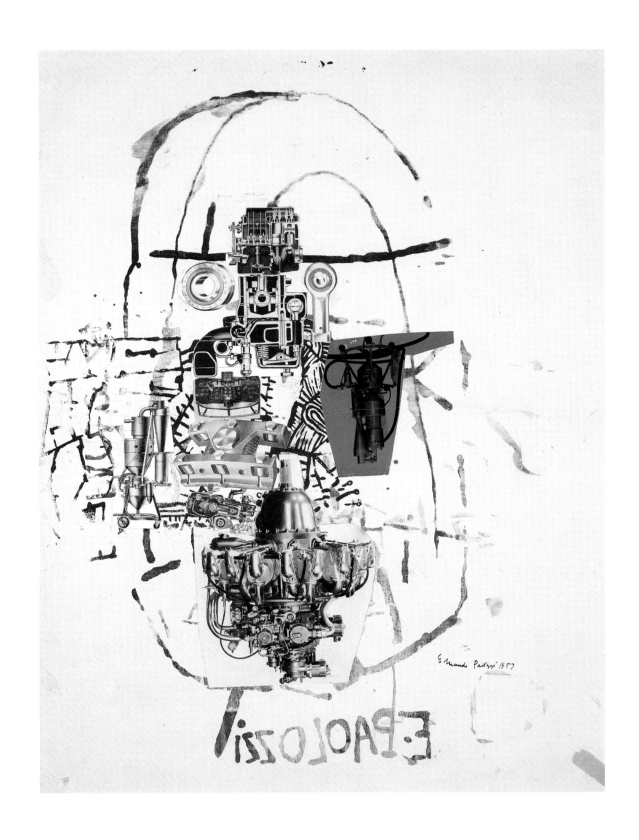

33

KENNETH ARMITAGE b. 1916
Figure lying on its side (Version V) 1957

bronze
82 long
purchased May 1958

'Each work of mine has, I hope, a formal or sculptural idea, which, however simple, is the first-stage conscious reason for its existence. But intimately linked with this is something else which I find hard to define – an instinctive concern with a human condition or attitude either trivial, serious, ambiguous or obvious. When this is quite absent I am lost or bored. For this reason it is sometimes not of first importance if the work is large or small, nor even what the material it is or how it is made, but it is certainly essential that there are (even token) figurative associations. Once or twice I have moved away from figurative work only to flee quickly back again...'

Kenneth Armitage, Arts Council of Great Britain, 1972 – 73

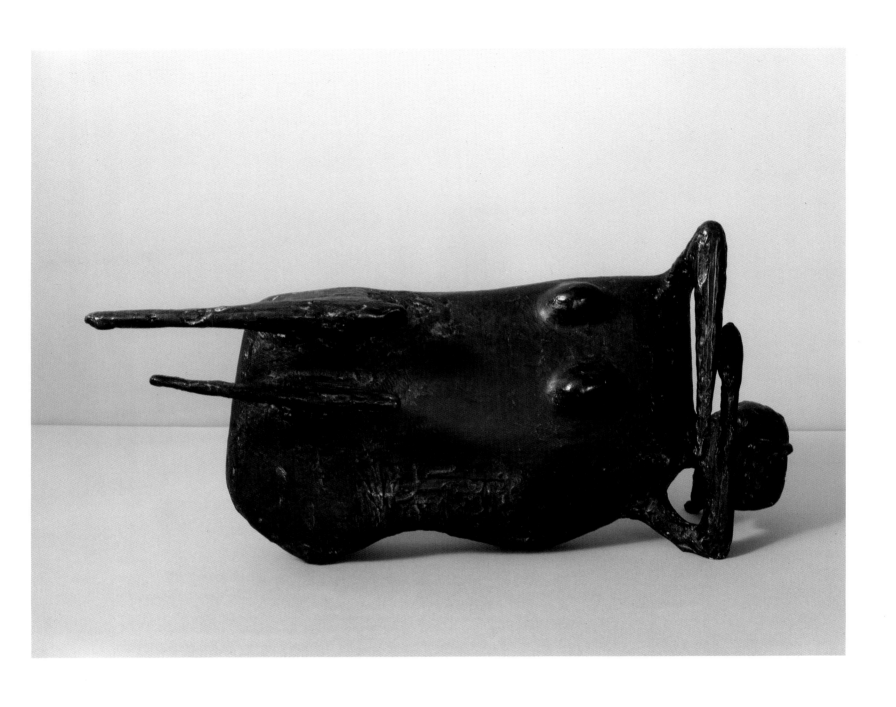

34

DAVID HOCKNEY b. 1937
Man in a museum (or *You're in the wrong movie*) 1962

oil on canvas

147 × 152.4

purchased August 1971

'I never seem to be able to go around a museum at the same pace as anybody else, and when I went to the Pergamon Museum with Jeff we got separated. Suddenly I caught sight of him standing next to an Egyptian sculpted figure, unconcerned about it because he was studying something on the wall. Both figures were looking the same way, and it amused me that in my first glimpse of them they looked united. In the painting, the husband stands politely, and the sculpture is made to look like his wife who is a bit tired and therefore sitting down. They're both looking at the same thing, but we can't see it. As the scene in the museum focused for me, it seemed all the more amusing because the connection between the two figures was so tenuous.'

David Hockney by David Hockney, Thames and Hudson, 1976

83

35

EDUARDO PAOLOZZI b. 1924
Diana as an Engine 1963 – 66

welded and painted aluminium
193.7 × 97.5 × 53.3
purchased March 1963

'I suppose I am interested, above all, in investigating the golden ability
of the artist to achieve a metamorphosis of quite ordinary things into
something wonderful and extraordinary that is neither nonsensical nor
morally edifying… It is the sublime of everyday life. I seek to stress all
that is wonderful or ambiguous in the most ordinary objects, in fact
often in objects that nobody stops to look at or admire. Besides, I try to
subject these objects, which are the basic materials of my sculptures, to
more than one metamorphosis. Generally, I am conscious, as I work,
of seeking to achieve two or at most three changes in my materials, but
sometimes I then discover that I have unconsciously achieved a fourth
or even a fifth metamorphosis too. That is why I believe that an artist
who works with *objets trouvés* must avoid being dominated by his
materials. Wonderful as these may be, they are not endowed with a
mind and cannot, as the artist often does, change their mind as they are
being transformed. On the contrary, the artist must dominate his
materials completely, so as to fully transform or transmute them.'

Dialogues on Art, Edouard Roditi, Secker and Warburg, 1960

36
PHILLIP KING b. 1934
Brake 1966

fibreglass
213.4 × 366 × 488
purchased February 1968

'There is a spiral movement in *Brake* reminiscent of the tradition of form in the round (Bernini etc.). The spiral in its movement describes a cone – I was in a way retracing for myself and within my own work the earlier historical path of sculpture from volume to internal reduced structural forms… part of the attraction of the piece for me was the constant section of the form. It meant I could use the same mould for different parts.'

From an interview with Lynne Cooke, *Phillip King,* Arts Council of Great Britain, 1981

37
PATRICK CAULFIELD b. 1936
View inside a Cave 1966

oil on board
122 × 213.4
purchased March 1968

''View inside a cave' was one of a number of paintings with the prefix "View". They were emphatically horizontal "landscape" shaped paintings suggesting the concept of a view. The title being partly ironic as the paintings were painted in a flat shadowless manner that denied the recessive expectations of a view.

'The idea of the "View" paintings simply provided a starting point for a few unlikely images from the imagination'.

Artist to the Curator, March 1990

38

BRIDGET RILEY b. 1931

Cataract 3 1967

emulsion PVA on linen
221.9 × 222.9
purchased February 1968

'I draw from nature. I work with nature, although in completely new terms. For me nature is not landscape, but the dynamism of visual forces – an event rather than an appearance – these forces can only be tackled by treating colour and form as ultimate identities, freeing them from all descriptive or functional roles.'

British Drawings and Watercolours, The British Council, 1982

39
ANTHONY CARO b. 1924
Pink Stack 1969

painted steel
320.2 × 117 × 162.5
purchased September 1969

'I'm not interested in monuments. I'm fed up with objects on pedestals. I'd like to break down the graspability of sculpture.'

From an interview with Lawrence Alloway, *Gazette,* 1, 1961

'All sculptors have dreams of defying gravity. One of the inherent qualities about sculpture is its heaviness, its substance. There is an attraction in the dream of putting heavy pieces calmly up in the air and getting them to stay there…if you can make the floor act as part of the sculpture, and not just the base, then the pieces will float and move anyway. I would like to make sculptures that are more abstract. Sculpture of its nature is not as abstract as painting…. The old statue was made on a base and it inhabited a world of its own, the limits of which were set by the limits of its base. I don't want my sculpture to relate to the spectator in this imaginary sort of way. It has to do with presence, more as one person relates to another.'

From an interview with Phyllis Tuchman, *Artforum,* New York, June 1972

40

SEAN SCULLY b. 1945
Red Light 1972

acrylic on canvas

274.4 × 183

purchased March 1973

'I'm interested in art that addresses itself to our highest aspirations. That's why I can't do figurative painting – I think figurative painting's ultimately trivial now. It's all humanism and no form.

'Abstraction's the art of our age. It's a breaking down of certain structures, an opening up. It allows you to think without making oppressively specific references, so that the viewer is free to identify with the work. Abstract art has the possibility of being incredibly generous, really out there for everybody. It's a non-denominational religious art. I think it's the spiritual art of our time.'

From an interview with Sean Scully by Judith Higgins, *Art News,* November 1985

41

RICHARD SMITH b. 1931

Three Squares 2 1975

acrylic on canvas with aluminium rods and string

3 canvas, 175 × 175 each

purchased March 1976

'When an idea cannot be made visible within the terms I use, I recognize that conventions have been set up. The conventions then have to be broken… When you paint across something that is three-dimensional, the third dimensional reality is too strong for extra play with added illusion. You are severely restricted to painting what you've got.'

Richard Smith Recent Work 1972 – 1977, MIT, Cambridge, Mass., 1978

42
JEFFERY CAMP b. 1923
Beachy Head – Dawn 1975 – 84

oil on canvas on board
121.9 × 121.9
inscribed lre: Camp
purchased March 1984

'The wind blows on the South Coast, one horizon never seems enough: a succession of bars, framing the vastness implies recession, the sheer drop. Like a gyro top, a picture on its point. Beachy Head is very high – like mountaineering but without the danger it makes the second by second dying of thoughts more intense. Like gulls dropping from cliffs, like leaps of consciousness, like quick film rushes towards death. In this lies the perennial attraction of this well-known beauty spot.'

Jeffery Camp: a retrospective exhibition of paintings, South London Art Gallery, 1973

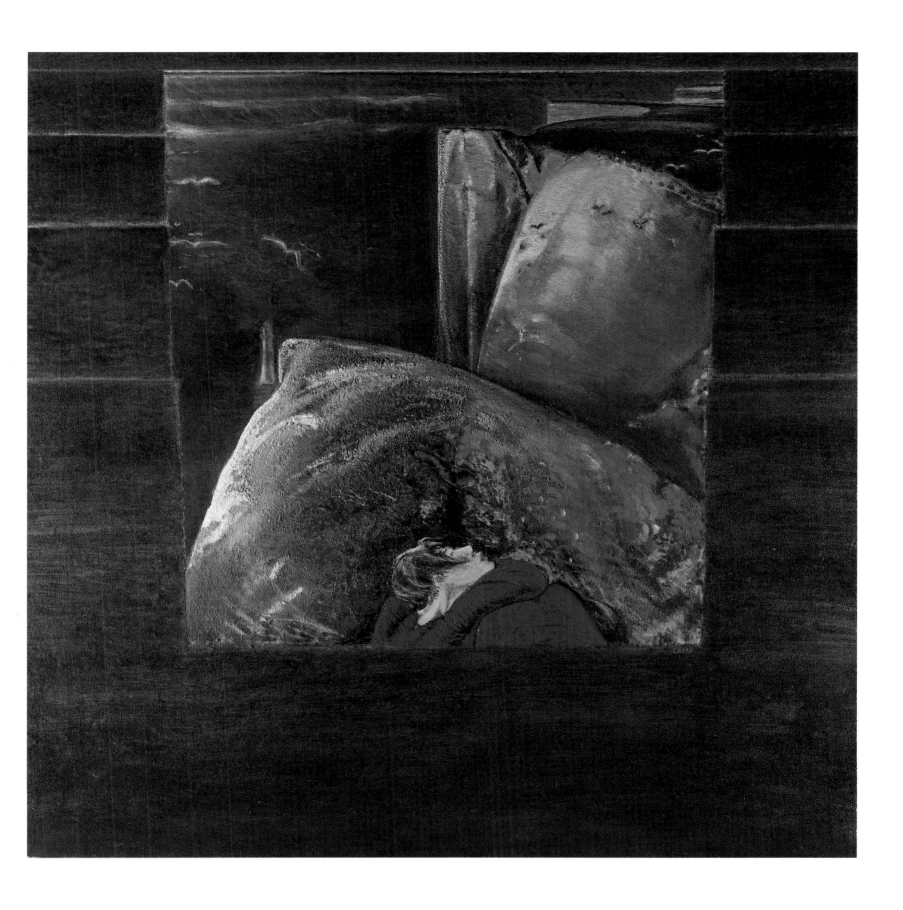

43

HOWARD HODGKIN b. 1932
Still Life in a Restaurant 1976 – 79

oil on wood
92.7 × 118.1
purchased March 1987

'As far as the subject of my picture goes, they are about one moment of time involving particular people in relationship to each other and also to me. After that moment has occurred all the problems are pictorial. My pictures have become more elaborate because I want them to contain more of the subject, but to me the paramount difficulty is to make the picture into as finite and solid an object as possible in physical terms and to include nothing irrelevant or confusing; ideally they should be like materials.'

From a recorded talk on his paintings, British Council, 1976

44

Richard Long b. 1945
Stone Line 1979

Cornish slate
239 × 130
purchased February 1980

I like simple, practical emotional,
quiet, vigorous art.

I like the simplicity of walking,
the simplicity of stones.

I like common materials, whatever is to hand,
but especially stones. I like the idea that stones
are what the world is made of.

I like common means given the
simple twist of art.

I like sensibility without technique.

I like the way the degree of visibility
and accessibility of my art is controlled
by circumstance, and also the degree to which
it can be either public or private,
possessed or not possessed.

I like to use the symmetry of patterns between time,
places and time, between distance and time,
between stones and distance, between time and stones.

I choose lines and circles because they
do the job.

Five, six, pick up sticks
Seven, eight, lay them straight
Anthony d'Offay Gallery, 1980

45
GILBERT AND GEORGE b. 1943 and 1942
Intellectual Depression 1980

photo-piece (16 panels)
242 × 202 (overall size)
purchased February 1981

'We invented and we are constantly developing our own visual language. We want the most accessible modern form with which to create the most modern speaking visual pictures of our time. The art-material must be subservient to the meaning and purpose of the picture. Our reason for making pictures is to change people and not to congratulate them on being how they are.

True Art comes from three main life-forces. They are: –

THE HEAD
THE SOUL
and THE SEX

In our life these forces are shaking and moving themselves into ever-changing different arrangements. Each one of our pictures is a frozen representation of one these "arrangements".'

The Art of Gilbert and George, Wolf Jahn, Thames and Hudson, 1989

INTELLECTUAL
DEPRESSION
Gilbert and *George*
1980

46

FRANK AUERBACH b. 1931
Head of JYM III 1980

oil on board
71.1 × 61
purchased January 1985

'There's a phrase by Robert Frost about his verse, I don't know what it means about verse, and I really barely comprehend what it suggests about painting, but it seems to me to be absolutely true. He said, "I want a poem to be like ice on a stove – riding on its own melting". Well, a great painting is like ice on a stove. It is a shape riding on its own melting into matter and space, it never stops moving backwards and forwards.'

From an interview with Catherine Lampert, *Frank Auerbach,* Arts Council of Great Britain, 1978

47

LUCIAN FREUD b. 1922
Naked girl with egg 1980 – 81

oil on canvas
75 × 60.5
purchased March 1982

'When I look at a body I know it gives me choices of what to put in a painting; what will suit me and what won't. There is a distinction between fact and trust. Trust has an element of revelation about it… I used to leave the face until last. I wanted the expression to be in the body. The head must be just another limb. So I had to play down expression in the nudes… One of the ways in which I could get them to sit was by involving them…the painting is always done very much with their co-operation. The problem with painting a nude, of course, is that it deepens the transaction. You can scrap a painting of someone's face and it imperils the sitter's self-esteem less than scrapping a painting of the whole naked body. We know our faces after all. We see them every day, out there at large in the mirror or the photo. But we don't scrutinize our bodies to the same degree, unless we are professional models, whom I don't use, or extreme narcissists, whom I can't use.'

Lucian Freud, The British Council, 1987

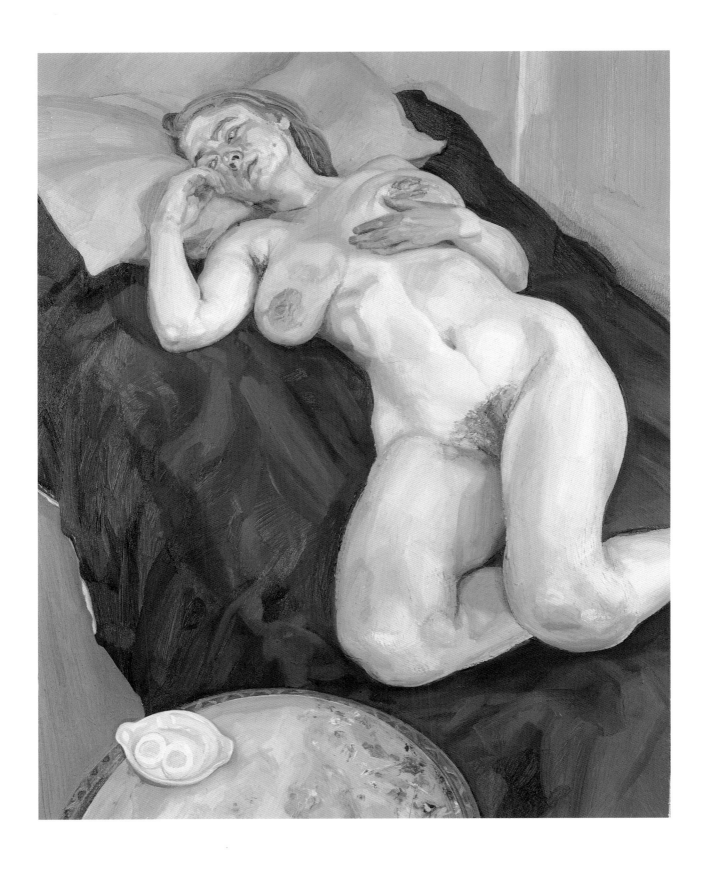

48
Barry Flanagan b. 1941
Cricketer 1981

bronze
156.2 × 39.3 × 53.4
purchased March 1982

'I seem to pursue shape and form as an abstract constituent in sculpture almost exclusively in stone, whereas the bronze work is the result of another set of ideas, really: the themes are evocative of a human situation or activity. And the chosen subject, the surrogate figure, is the hare. These beasts are always doing something sporting in one way or another.

'Thematically the choice of the hare is really quite a rich and expressive sort of mode – the conventions of the cartoon and the investment of human attributes into the animal world is a very well practiced device, in literature and film, etcetera, and is really quite poignant. And on a practical level, if you consider what conveys situation and meaning and feeling in a human figure, the range of expression is in fact far more limited than the device of investing an animal – a hare especially – with the expressive attributes of a human being. The ears, for instance, are really able to convey far more than a squint in an eye of a figure, or a grimace on the face of a model.

'The actual figure – the figure of the hare – is described in the armature. Now there's very little drawing that's going to help you stitch, weld an armature together. You've got to do it there and then, weld it here, bend it there, to make an armature that's going to be the vehicle, and of course the content has to be in that armature before you begin work. So, that's where the drawing takes place, in space, in the workshop itself.'

From an interview with Judith Bumpus, *Barry Flanagan at the Whitechapel,* Whitechapel Art Gallery, 1983

49

RICHARD DEACON b. 1949
Boys and girls (come out to play) 1982

lino and plywood
91 × 183 × 152.5
purchased March 1983

'As a boy, always aware both of the possibility of imminent cataclysmic disaster and of the desire to leave, I used to keep a small case ready at hand under the bed. Among the things it contained – false documents, money, food, whistle, knife, string, etc – was a map. It was map I had drawn. The map had no relation to where I was. Evidently, I knew where I was, but would be going somewhere else, to a place I did not know. In such a place a map is useful. The map as I remember had a shape – as if it were the map of an island – with a few notional features. Shape is the outside edge, boundary, extremity, limit. It is other. By contrast, a street plan has no shape separate from the sheet on which it is printed. There is an implied continuity between the map and the place in which one stands. Somehow, therefore, in order for my map to represent another place in the intended sense, there was a necessity for it to have a shape or boundary. The contour of the interior, however, is always difficult.'

Richard Deacon 10 sculptures 1987 – 1989 ARC, Musée d'Art Moderne de la Ville de Paris, 1989

50

Richard Long b. 1945
Three Moors, Three Circles 1982

text on paper
103 × 153
purchased December 1988

I have in general been interested in using the
landscape in different ways from
traditional representation and the fixed view.
Walking, ideas, statements and maps are some means to this end.
I have tried to add something of my own view as an
artist to the wonderful and undisputed traditions
of walking, journeying and climbing. Thus, some
of my walks have been formal (straight,
circular) almost ritualised. The patterns of
my walks are unique and original; they
are not like following well-trodden routes
taking travellers from one place to another.
I have sometimes climbed around mountains
instead of to the top. I have used riverbeds
as footpaths. I have made walks about slowness, walks about
stones and water. I have made walks within
a place as opposed to a linear journey;
walking without travelling.

Words after the fact.

Five, six pick up sticks
Seven, eight, lay them straight
Anthony d'Offay Gallery, 1980

THREE MOORS   THREE CIRCLES

A 108 MILE WALK FROM BODMIN MOOR, TO DARTMOOR, TO EXMOOR,
WALKING AROUND THREE CIRCLES ALONG THE WAY

LISKEARD TO PORLOCK

51

ANISH KAPOOR b. 1954
The Chant of Blue 1983

polystyrene, resin, gesso and pigment (in four pieces)
3 pieces: 61 × 61 × 61; 1 piece 76 × 76 × 76
purchased July 1983

On a visit to his native India in 1979:

'Outside some of the temples there they sell powder colour which is used in the temple ritual. Looking at it I thought about making sculpture. It seemed like an answer to a problem. Why paint something when it could be made out of colour?…

'The first pieces were all red and white. Red pigment is like earth. It is phenomenological. That impressed me. I was investigating the phenomenon of redness. All the forms I made were towards that end. I then made some yellow works. I felt yellow was the passionate part of red, closely and very specifically allied to red – red being the centre. Colour is the idea, the problem is to give it form. While red is earth, it can also be fire and then I connect it with creative energy. I think I see it as the colour of my creativity. Later I made works out of blue pigment which, of course, is the colour of that which is disembodied. I think that while I was making blue pieces I was trying to reach this quality. Still later I made some blacks works. Black, like red, is earthy, but is more like the "dreadful mother", both creative and destructive. It is this symbolic nature of colour which is tied to real things that captivated me then, and is still a driving force.'

Anish Kapoor on Paper 1975 – 1987, Ray Hughes Gallery, Queensland, Australia, 1988

52
Bill Woodrow b. 1948
Long Distance Information 1983

metal and mixed media
180 × 104 × 38
purchased March 1983

Based on Chuck Berry's popular song of the 1960's, *Long Distance Information* (celebrating the possibility of talking to a child by telephone across a continent):

'Ree is only six years old, Information, please, help me get in touch with her in Memphis, Tennessee.'

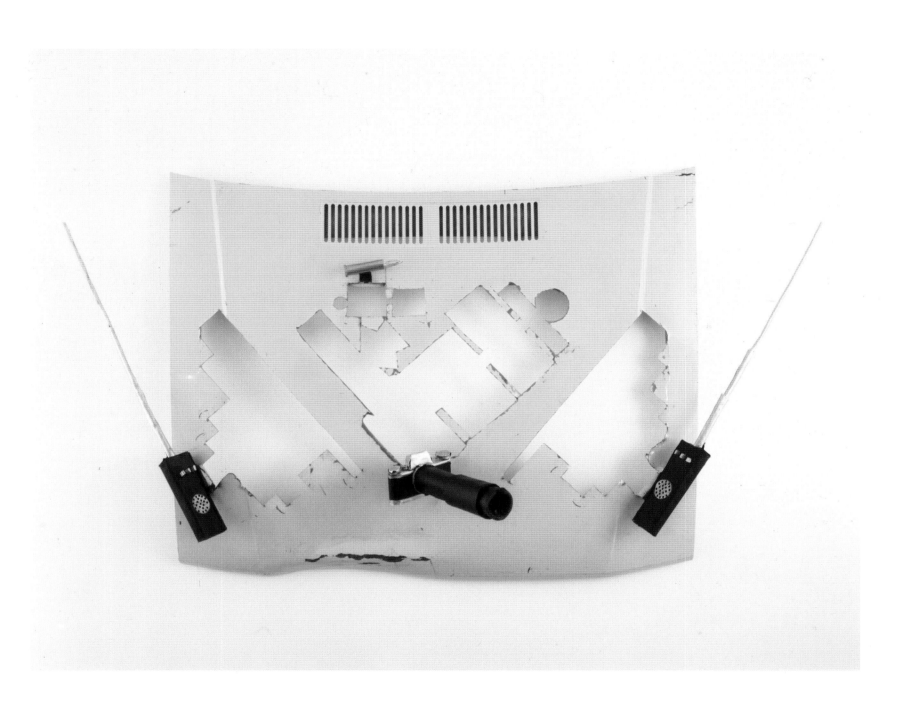

53
FRANK AUERBACH b. 1931
Tree on Primrose Hill 1984 – 5

oil on canvas
122.6 × 148.6
purchased March 1986

Q: Is it a very different kind of experience, painting a figure and painting a landscape where you have to make a sketch and travel between the spot and the studio to some degree?

A: 'There are two great differences. One of them is that when I work from a model there is a person in the room. The person creates her own urgency by being present, that is, she has come to be painted. Occasionally if the situation is an intimate one, there are other urgencies which are created. Of course, each sitter in a sense creates, to some extent, a unique atmosphere, so that one finds oneself behaving differently because the sitter's a different person. I think that my sitters would tell you that I'm usually fairly abandoned when they're there, but there's a further degree of abandon when I'm doing the landscape because I'm absolutely on my own. And what is more, I actually find the landscapes, although they're not enormous, tremendous physical effort because that particular size and the way I work means putting up a whole image, and dismantling it and putting up another whole image, which is actually physically extremely strenuous, and I don't think I've ever finished a landscape without a six or seven hour bout of work. Whereas, a person or a head is a single form and it can come about in a shorter period of time. I think about working outside on landscapes. It's not so much a question of temperate climate, it's just the question of the paraphernalia is insoluble, and the idea of working in public in the ludicrous way that I do work would be just unacceptable to me.'

From an interview with Catherine Lampert, *Frank Auerbach,* Arts Council of Great Britain, 1978

54
Leon Kossoff b. 1926
Christchurch, Spitalfields 1987

oil on canvas
61.5 × 56
purchased October 1988

'Moved, I suppose, by the extraordinary first few chapters of Peter Ackroyd's book *Hawksmoor,* I walked once again down Brick Lane towards Christchurch, Spitalfields, a building which like St Paul's has always been a part of my life. I have tried to draw Christchurch twice before. The first time was about thirty years ago when I returned to live in Bethnal Green, the second time about fifteen years ago when I shared a studio in Dalston with some ex-students. Both attempts were failures. It seems that time has to pass, that we have to change in some way, before certain subjects become accessible to us. Fortunately, Christchurch is still with us, and, in the dusty sunlight of this August day, when this part of London still looks and feels like the London of Blake's Jerusalem, I find myself involved once again in making drawings and the idea for a painting begins to emerge. The urgency that drives me to work is not only to do with the pressure of the accumulation of memories and the unique quality of the subject on this particular day but also with the awareness that time is short, that soon the mass of this building will be dwarfed by more looming office blocks and overshadowed, the character of the structure will be lost forever, for it is by its monumental flight into unimpeded space that we remember this building.'

'From a letter to a student who was asking about my involvement with subjects outside the studio, 1986.'

Leon Kossoff, Anthony d'Offay Gallery, London, 1988

55
TONY CRAGG b. 1949
Mothers Milk II 1988

bronze

90 × 192 × 142

purchased December 1988

'I want people to stand there and think "This is a sculpture, how do I get involved with this sculpture?" I want objects to stand there just like they should be there, like they have actually earned their place. So that it's a self-understood thing that they are there and that they have a particular visual quality. They're there and they want a dialogue on the basis of all the other things that are in the world, and not on the basis of a particular group of objects which one has called, in the past, "sculpture". That's a fundamental tenet of my approach of making sculpture. So one has to be very aware of formal qualities. For me a sculpture will only work if its form is right. But I believe that as part of an investigation of the world and a deeper understanding of it, one can work towards a picture language that reveals sentiments and ideas which one has never had before. I have to couple this with what I said previously, that the object world as it stands, at the moment, is not being created with enough deep thought and care; there's not enough attention to it. If we're making a mess of things like polluting the world, that's relatively simple to stop; it's something else that concerns me more. To live in a world that had become predominantly artificial and man-made. That I can accept as long as the man-made world is providing images and meanings which are just as deep and meaningful as those which are found with naturally occurring things. So that, for example, when the tigers die out, as the dragons did, there will be something equivalent to take their place. If one wants to hear the radio in preference to bird-song, if it has values that one can accept, fine, but I think then one has really to develop its potential.'

Tony Cragg in conversation with Lynne Cooke, *Tony Cragg,* Arts Council of Great Britain, London, 1987

56
BOYD WEBB b. 1947
Corral 1989

unique colour photograph
158 × 123
purchased November 1989

'A tournament without victors.'

Artist to the Curator, March 1990

57
Patrick Caulfield b. 1936
The Blue Posts, 1989

acrylic on canvas
289.5 × 205.7
purchased March 1990

'The Blue Posts' refers to yet another public house of that name. It is an establishment without particular distinction or charm, but conveniently close to my London studio.

'The suggestion of colour and object in the title was appealing in that they are absent from the painting, which, however, still retains a visual association with the place itself. The painting is an analogy of this place constructed from various other sources and memories.'

Artist to the Curator, March 1990

58

BILL WOODROW b. 1948
Point of Entry 1989

cardboard into bronze
36 × 283 × 94
purchased March 1990

MUM

child's and /or familiar word for mother.

DAD

child's and/or familiar word for father.

CHILD

product of a mother and a father.

WAR

quarrel, often between nations, that is conducted by military force. There are at present wars or armed conflicts in the following countries: – Afghanistan, Angola, Bangladesh, Burma, Cambodia, Chad, Colombia, East Timor, Salvador, Ethiopia, Guatemala, India, Iran, Iraq, Israel, Lebanon, Morocco, Mozambique, Namibia, Nicaragua, Pakistan, Panama, Peru, Philippines, Somalia, South Africa, Soviet Union, Sri Lanka, Sudan, Turkey, United Kingdom.

DEAD FLESH

the currency of wars.

POINT OF ENTRY

a medical/military term for the exact position where a bullet strikes and enters a human body. Very often a relatively small, neat wound in comparison to those made internally or in the exit area.

Artist to the Curator, March 1990

59
R B KITAJ b. 1932
Melancholy after Dürer 1989

oil on canvas

123.5 × 122.5

purchased March 1990

'I have always considered myself a melancholic and assumed this temperament derived from my Russian grandparents. 1989 was a bad year and, after a heart attack, I fell into a slump. My friend Arikha told me to paint my depression and so I looked at the greatest image of this theme, Dürer's engraving, which I found in Panofsky's Dürer book which I have kept with me since teenage. Of course I have not done Dürer justice, but that is in keeping with what Panofsky says the print is about: "the tragic unrest of human creation". His text is remarkable and its theses wove in and around my poor painting while I stared at the print. The dog is traditionally associated with Melancholy and I painted my dog black because I was reading about Churchill's lifelong depression, which he called his "black dog". I repeated Dürer's contrast between the inertia of the Melancholic and the happily scribbling putto (my five-year-old Max). Panofsky says that we have no right to assume that every detail has a special "meaning", so I won't bore you further, except to say that the obliterated image at the lower left is a reminder of the constant failure of those of us who are so much less than Dürer, that same Dürer who said: "Even our groping will fail".'

Artist to the Curator, March 1990

60

HELEN CHADWICK b. 1953
Meat Abstracts 1989

colour polaroid prints (4), framed and mounted in silk matt
50.8 × 61 (each)
purchased January 1990

'These lamps are about being in flesh, pared down to the reciprocality of energy and matter that is "living meat". At its most bald, this is our flesh-hood – an "unstable cupola" tracing continua of separation and union that is the erotic corollary of our coming into being. Duration makes moments of coupling all too finite. To compensate, all we have is exchange, the heat of our physicality as impulse to activity, a bestial reason to counter the ruptive forces of mind and money valued over body.'

Helen Chadwick, *Lamps*, Marlene Eleine Gallery, 1989

Meat Abstract #4   Arthur Chadwick 4/4

BIOGRAPHIES OF THE ARTISTS
and
SELECTED BIBLIOGRAPHY

KENNETH ARMITAGE   b. 1916

Born in Leeds, Armitage studied at Leeds College of Art from 1934 – 37, then for two years at the Slade School. After the war he taught at the Bath Academy of Art as Head of Sculpture (1946 – 56).

Armitage destroyed nearly all his pre-war carvings and subsequently used plaster, later cast into bronze. He began creating groups of figures involved in casual everyday activities such as going for a walk, or sitting down on a bench, in which bodies appear as flat sheets, with limbs projecting almost like distress signals. He was one of three British representatives at the Venice Biennale of 1958 where he won the award for the best sculptor under forty-five and where the term "geometry of fear" was coined by Herbert Read to describe the particular flavour of this post-war British sculpture. The human figure continued to occupy a central part of his work until the late 70s when he turned, in his "Richmond Oaks" series, to non-figurative subjects.

A retrospective exhibition was held at the Whitechapel Art Gallery in 1959 and a survey exhibition was toured by the Arts Council in 1972 – 73. Between 1967 – 69 he was guest artist for the City of Berlin "Kunstlerprogramm", and in 1970, visiting Professor at Boston University, USA.

SELECTED BIBLIOGRAPHY

1. *Kenneth Armitage.*
Whitechapel Art Gallery, London 1959.

2. *Kenneth Armitage.*
Arts Council of Great Britain, London 1972 – 73.

FRANK AUERBACH b. 1931

Born in Berlin, the son of Jewish parents, Frank Auerbach was despatched to Britain in 1939 and educated at a country boarding-school; he never saw his parents again.

In 1947, the year he acquired British citizenship, he moved to London and took evening classes under David Bomberg at the Borough Polytechnic. In 1952 he entered the Royal College of Art, then taught in various London arts schools. He eventually left teaching to concentrate on painting. He has worked in the same studio in Primrose Hill, North London, since 1954.

Auerbach chooses a deliberately narrow range of subjects – his immediate environment and portraits of close friends. A sense of the struggle to bring his subject into existence is inherent in much of his work: "What I'm not hoping to do is paint another picture because there are enough pictures in the world. I'm hoping to make a new thing for the world that remains in the mind like a new species of living thing."

His first one-man exhibition was at the Beaux-Arts Gallery in 1956; in 1978 a retrospective was organised by the Arts Council. Together with Francis Bacon, Lucian Freud (q.v.), Leon Kossoff (q.v.) and R. B. Kitaj (q.v.) he has become identified as one of the leading figures of the 'School of London' (see K. B. Kitaj). In 1986 he represented Britain at the Venice Biennale where he was awarded the *Lion d'Or* (jointly with Sigmar Polke).

SELECTED BIBLIOGRAPHY

1. *Frank Auerbach.*
Arts Council of Great Britain, London 1978.

2. *Frank Auerbach: Paintings and Drawings 1977 – 1985, Venice Biennale.*
The British Council, London 1986.

EDWARD BURRA 1905 – 1976

Born in London, Burra suffered from chronic arthritis from early adolescence but he didn't let it inhibit his zest for travel or for the louche pleasures of the underworld. After studying at the Royal College of Art from 1923 – 25, he worked in watercolour, oils being too heavy for his already badly crippled body. Despite virtual confinement to his Sussex home for the greater part of his life, he managed to visit Paris and the South of France, where he found inspiration in the music halls, bars and brothels. In 1923 he travelled to North America and Mexico, enjoying the jazz clubs of Harlem and the disreputable dives of Mexico in a way that appealed to his sense of subversion: 'Englishmen' wouldn't normally frequent such places. During the 1930s his work became increasingly concerned with sinister juxtaposition (much learned from Mexico), and he participated in Unit One (q.v. Paul Nash) and the International Surrealist Exhibition in London in 1936. His work was deeply affected by the Spanish Civil War.

After World War II, Burra's interest shifted to still life and later, to the English landscape. These he treated as disturbed idylls. A retrospective was held at the Tate Gallery in 1973, and a second at the Hayward Gallery, London in 1985.

SELECTED BIBLIOGRAPHY

1. *Edward Burra.*
Arts Council of Great Britain, London 1985.

2. *Well, dearie: The Complete Letters of Edward Burra.*
Edited by William Chappell. Gordon Fraser, London 1985.

JEFFERY CAMP b. 1923

Born at Oulton Broad, Suffolk, Camp was educated locally at Ipswich School of Art before moving to Edinburgh College of Art in 1941. He returned to Suffolk in 1944, to paint the bitter East Anglian coastline: 'Fishing life was more dangerous than mining'. He was awarded several travelling scholarships and from 1963 – 1989 taught at the Slade School. By the time of his first one-man shown in 1959 (at the Beaux Art Gallery), his preoccupations were unmistakable: the possession of a particular landscape, a landscape of horizons and meeting points, where land meets sea, sea meets sky. In 1963 his marriage to a half-Chinese painter, Laetitia Yhap, defined the focus further: the meeting of finite and infinite, limits and limitlessness, as her half-Chinese features are explored against the precipitous chalk-face on the South Coast of England at *Beachy Head*, famous both as a beauty and a suicide spot. In 1982 Camp brought out a widely acclaimed book, *Draw*, which emphasised his status as a phenomenal draughtsman. 'Drawing can open the door and raise that useful extra eyelid, which like that possessed by certain lizards, is in humans the inhibiting, cribbed, confining, narrow-browed, vertical thinking curtain eyelid of conformity,' Camp was elected a Royal Academician in 1984 and had a major retrospective at the Royal Academy in 1988. More recently his work has featured the river life of the Thames as it flows through central London.

SELECTED BIBLIOGRAPHY

1. *Jeffery Camp*.
South London Art Gallery, London 1973.

2. *Jeffery Camp: Paintings 1949 – 1988*.
Exeter City Museums Service and Tyne and Wear Museums Service 1988.

3. *Draw – How to Master the Art* by Jeffery Camp.
Andre Deutsch, London 1981.

ANTHONY CARO b. 1924

Born in New Malden, Surrey, Caro read engineering at Cambridge, followed by two years in the Navy from 1946 – 47. He studied sculpture at the Regent Street Polytechnic and from 1947 – 52 at the Royal Academy School.

A part-time assistant to Henry Moore (q.v.) he began to model in clay and his early figures in bronze reflect his interests in the work of painters such as Bacon and Dubuffet, as well as Picasso's sculpture.

Caro's friendship with the American critic Clement Greenberg refined his ideas on sculpture and following a Ford Foundation scholarship in New York he turned to making abstract constructed sculptures. He was the first to create large sculptures that spread along the ground independent of base or pedestal. This innovation broke with the "totemic" conventions of Western sculpture. Many of his sculptures were brightly painted to emphasise their mood and those of the late 1960s were marked by great inventiveness, several having associations with landscape.

While Caro's work extended the tradition of constructed sculpture, His contribution was no less significant, and his methods at St Martin's School of Art became an important catalyst for a younger generation: Flanagan (q.v.) Long (q.v.) and Gilbert and George (q.v.) were among his students.

Caro's first retrospective took place at the Hayward Gallery, London, in 1969, followed by another at the Museum of Modern Art, New York, in 1975. He was knighted in 1987.

SELECTED BIBLIOGRAPHY

1. *Anthony Caro*.
Museum of Modern Art, New York 1975.

2. *Anthony Caro: Sculpture 1969 – 84*.
Arts Council of Great Britain, London 1984.

PATRICK CAULFIELD b. 1936

Born in London, Patrick Caulfield studied at Chelsea School of Art from 1956 – 1960 and at the Royal College of Art from 1960 – 63.

Although identified as one of the 'Pop' generation during the 60s, Caulfield's subject matter has little in common with that of his contemporaries who favoured popular imagery culled from the mass media. Instead, Caulfield chose to re-work and 'modernize' the traditional themes of Western art, such as the still-life, the interior and the Mediterranean view. His work is marked as much by irony and his delight in visual cliché as for its clear 'commercial' colour and thick black outlines which were, until recently, a hallmark of his style. His own interpretation of his work is that, 'it began as a wholesale reaction against sensitive Slade School English painting which believed that it was bad taste to finish anything'.

He taught at Chelsea School of Art from 1963 for eight years, but subsequently has devoted himself to painting and printmaking. A retrospective exhibition was held at the Walker Art Gallery, Liverpool, and the Tate Gallery, London, in 1981.

SELECTED BIBLIOGRAPHY

1. *Patrick Caulfield* by Christopher Finch.
Penguin Books, Middlesex 1971.

2. *Patrick Caulfield: Paintings 1962 – 81*.
Tate Gallery, London 1981.

HELEN CHADWICK b. 1953

Helen Chadwick's contribution to contemporary art has been both original and intensely personal, characterised by the use of her own body as both subject and object. Few artists have embraced the means of modern technology – the photocopier, light projection, polaroid and recently, the computer and microscope – in such a distinctive way.

After studying at Brighton Polytechnic from 1973 – 76 and Chelsea School of Art from 1976 – 77, she began to make soft, organic objects based on parts of her body. Direct and intimate, she translated these sculptures into live performances.

Early autobiographical works depicted her development from birth to maturity. Later more complex installations comprised photocopied images of her body suspended in a sea of organic forms and decay, emphasising the sensuality and transience of physical pleasure.

A constant theme in much of Chadwick's work has been the questioning of boundaries – both physical and cultural. A series of 'viral landscape' photoworks involved a computer generation of Chadwick's cellular structure overlaid onto images of natural coastline. Her most recent work, using the polaroid, presents the viscera of the body in an extraordinary examination of the function, form and fetish of internal organs.

Chadwick was shortlisted for the Turner Prize in 1987.

SELECTED BIBLIOGRAPHY

1. *Of Mutability: Helen Chadwick.*
Institute of Contemporary Arts, London 1986.

2. *Enfleshings: Helen Chadwick* by Marina Warner.
Secker and Warburg, London 1989.

TONY CRAGG b. 1949

Born in Liverpool, Cragg worked as a lab technician for two years (1966 – 68) before turning to formal art education. At Wimbledon School of Art (1969 – 72) he began to experiment with materials not commonly regarded as those of the traditional sculptor. He studied at the Royal College of Art from 1973 – 77, where Richard Deacon (q.v.) was a student, and also formed friendships with Richard Long (q.v.) and Bill Woodrow (q.v.) during this period. He continues to live and work in Wuppertal, West Germany, after moving there in 1977 with his German wife.

Cragg's early works in plastic established his emergent vocabulary of materials, objects and images, using the floor or, from 1980, the wall as a base. He quickly displayed an innovative use of wide range of diverse materials, handled with an inventiveness which has opened up a new territory for sculpture, dealing with a predominantly urban environment which Cragg calls 'the new nature'.

Cragg has exhibited internationally since the late 1970s. In 1988 he represented Britain at the Venice Biennale and was also awarded the Turner Prize. The same year saw his appointment as Professor of Sculpture at the Kunstakademie, Düsseldorf, where he has taught since 1979.

SELECTED BIBLIOGRAPHY

1. *Tony Cragg*
Arts Council of Great Britain, London 1987.

2. *Tony Cragg – 1988 Venice Biennale*
British Council, London 1988.

RICHARD DEACON b. 1949

Born in Bangor, Wales, Richard Deacon moved to London where he studied at St Martin's School of Art from 1969 – 72. He studied at the Royal College of Art from 1974 – 77, where Tony Cragg (q.v.) was also a student, and later at the Chelsea School of Art (1977 – 78).

While in New York in 1978 – 79 with his wife, the ceramicist, Jacqui Poncelet, he began to make pots and drawings based on the "Sonnets to Orpheus" by Raine Maria Rilke. On his return to London, he made a group of works that employed swelling, curvilinear forms (fabricated at first from laminated wood) which have characterised much of his work since then. New materials, among them lino and galvanised steel, were introduced, and some works were industrially fabricated. The distinctive titles and configurations of many of his sculptures allude to organic forms.

A leading figure in contemporary British sculpture, Deacon has exhibited internationally throughout the 1980s. He has worked with architects (Richard Rogers) film-makers (John Tchalenko) and a dance company (Ballet Rambert) on numerous projects. He was awarded the Turner Prize in 1987.

SELECTED BIBLIOGRAPHY

1. *Richard Deacon: Sculpture 1980 – 84.*
Fruitmarket Gallery, Edinburgh 1984.

2. *Richard Deacon.*
Whitechapel Art Gallery, London 1988.

BARRY FLANAGAN b. 1944

Barry Flanagan was born in Prestatyn, North Wales. After a period at Birmingham College of Arts and Crafts, and various jobs, he enrolled as a student at St Martin's School of Art in 1964.

Flanagan's early use of 'poor' materials (sand, sacking, rope etc) opened up new possibilities for sculpture, but also reflected a keen wit, a lightness of touch and a feel for the stuff of things that have come to characterise all his work. By the late 1970s stone carving occupied a central area of interest: in 1978 he imported a three-ton stock of stone from Pietrasanta, Italy: 'something to get my teeth on.' In 1979 he began bronze casting. A much favoured subject in this medium has been the hare, though other animals – elephants, birds – have also been featured. A group of bronze horses cast in 1983 was inspired by the horses of San Marco in Venice, which he studied while they were under restoration in Venice in 1982.

Flanagan has exhibited widely since the 1970s. In 1982 he represented Britain at the Venice Biennale. In 1987/88 a survey exhibition was shown at Newcastle upon Tyne and was toured to Yugoslavia by the British Council.

SELECTED BIBLIOGRAPHY

1. *Barry Flanagan – Venice Biennale 1982.*
British Council, London 1982.

2. *Barry Flanagan: A Visual Invitation – Sculpture 1967 – 1987.*
Tyne and Wear Museums Service and the British Council, 1987.

LUCIAN FREUD b. 1922

Born in Berlin and grandson of the inventor of psychoanalysis, Freud left Germany with his family at the age of ten to settle in England. He studied briefly at the Central School of Art and at Goldsmiths College, and spent a short period at the art school run by Cedric Morris in Dedham, Suffolk.

After the war he settled in London, where he continues to live and work, painting people and places he knows intimately – such as the painting included here of his first wife, clutching a rose.

By the end of the 1950s a looser, more painterly technique had replaced his earlier graphic style. The portraits and studies of nudes produced since then have earned Freud acclaim as one of the most original painters of the late 20th century – original in the sense of innovation rather than novelty. Almost single-handed he has revived the language of figure and portrait painting in the post-war period. He is a leading figure of the group known as the 'School of London' (a term invented by R B Kitaj (q.v.)), and his work has concentrated almost exclusively on the single figure within the confines of his own central London studio.

A retrospective was organized by the Arts Council in 1974 and a large survey of his paintings toured to the United States, France, Germany and Britain by the British Council in 1987/88. Freud's graphics have also been the subject of recent exhibitions, notably *Works on Paper* (1988 – 89) organized by the Arts Council.

SELECTED BIBLIOGRAPHY

1. *Lucian Freud* by Lawrence Gowing.
Thames and Hudson, London 1982.

2. *Lucian Freud: Paintings.*
The British Council, London 1987.

3. *Lucian Freud: Works on Paper.*
South Bank Board, London 1988.

GILBERT AND GEORGE b. 1943 and 1942

Gilbert and George were born respectively in 1943 in the Dolomites, and in 1942 in Devon. They met in 1987 when they were both studying sculpture at St Martin's School of Art, and have lived and worked together presenting themselves as a single persona ever since.

Much of their early work was performed as 'living sculpture' in which they adopted various poses for several hours. The most famous of these was *Our New Sculpture* (1969), later retitled *Underneath the Arches*, 'sculpted' to a tape of a pre-war song about unemployment made famous by a music-hall duo, Flanagan and Allan.

A period spent in the country in summer 1970 was celebrated in several pieces of 'charcoal on paper sculptures' and later in the oil paintings, *The Paintings (with us in the nature)* (1971). Photographic pieces have gradually come to preoccupy them, although they continue to describe their work as sculpture. Highly personal, their work is often presented as an allegory of the urban world of modern man. Since the 1980s their work has largely been on an heroic scale and in heraldic colour, like stained glass.

Gilbert and George have exhibited internationally since the 1970s. In 1981 they made the film *The World of Gilbert and George*, which summarises their principal concerns. In 1990 an exhibition of their work will be staged in Moscow.

SELECTED BIBLIOGRAPHY

1. *Gilbert and George 1968 – 1980.*
Van Abbemuseum, Eindhoven 1980.

2. *The Art of Gilbert and George* by Wolf Jahn.
Thames and Hudson, London 1989.

HAROLD GILMAN 1876 – 1919

Born at Rode, Somerset Gilman was the son of an Anglican vicar. He spent a year in Odessa (1895) before beginning his training at Hastings School of Art in 1896, and attended the Slade School from 1897 – 1901.

Gilman's early career was frustrated by lack of financial and artistic success. In 1907 he met Sickert (q.v.) and became a founder member of the Fitzroy Street Group, later joining the Camden Town Group in 1911. Both groups advocated local 'unglamorous' subject matter and Gilman's work was strengthened by both associations. His concentration on domestic interiors, painted with subtle, unemphatic realism was a departure from the conventions of English painting at the time, as was his use of bright, pure colour. Under Sickert's influence he was encouraged to experiment with new subjects such as the nude and interiors, and he became a detached observer of the world of London eating-houses, furnished rooms, landladies and parlours of the mid Edwardian years: these subjects he made his own.

An impressive series of portraits from 1913 revealed Gilman's degree of psychological insight and sympathy, particularly for the denizens of working-class London, portrayed with a clear-eyed lack of sentimentality. In 1918 he received his first major commission from the Canadian Government to paint Halifax Harbour for the War Memorial in Ottawa. He died soon after its completion.

SELECTED BIBLIOGRAPHY

1. *Harold Gilman; An appreciation* by Wyndham Lewis.
Chatto and Windus, London 1919.

2. *Harold Gilman 1876 – 1919.*
Arts Council of Great Britain, London 1981.

SPENCER GORE 1878 – 1914

Despite his early death from pneumonia at the age of 35, Spencer Gore made a significant contribution to the course of English painting in the years before World War I. Born in Epsom, Surrey, he studied at the Slade School from 1896 – 1899 before making several visits to France, where he stayed in Sickert's house (q.v.) near Dieppe. The two painters would work separately by day, meeting in the evenings to discuss their work and their ideas for English art; Gore's quite personal assimilation of French Impressionism and Post-Impressionism was to be reflected in his original use of colour.

In 1905 Gore joined the Fitzroy Street circle of painters and under Sickert's encouragement painted a series of London theatre interiors, characterised by increasingly strong contrasts of colour. Despite a tendency to decorativeness, Gore's painting retained an emphatic sense of design, due in part to his habits of working from small, well documented drawings. Many of Gore's paintings during this period reflect his residence in and around Mornington Crescent (one of Camden Town's principal thoroughfares), its gardens and street façades. In 1911 he became a founder member of the Camden Town Group.

Gore's landscape paintings of Hertfordshire and later Richmond where he moved from Camden town in 1913 became increasingly boldly designed and flattened. He died at the outbreak of World War I.

SELECTED BIBLIOGRAPHY

1. *Spencer Frederick Gore 1878 – 1914.*
Arts Council of Great Britain, London 1955.

2. *Spencer Frederick Gore 1878 – 1914.*
Anthony d'Offay Gallery, London 1983.

ROGER HILTON 1911 – 1975

Born near London, Hilton studied at the Slade School from 1929 – 31 and in Paris until 1939. His service during World War II included three years as a prisoner-of-war. During the late 40s he worked among a small group of British artists interested in abstraction, particularly Peter Lanyon (q.v.) in Cornwall. He experimented with ways of depicting forms in space, first placing them in an illusory space, then as if on the surface alone, then as if floating in water. Despite the constant appeal of abstraction, his work never lost touch with the visual world. Allusions to the female torso are especially prevalent, and his frank humorous nudes always have pleasing abstract qualities. Confined to bed with poor health for some years during the 60s he started to draw animals and birds, allowing his imagination free play.

By 1974 he was confined to bed as an invalid precipitated in part by alcoholism, but never lost either his sense of humour or a certain combativeness: "As you live it changes the line you make. As your life is, so is your line. As you live it becomes more your line. The line says more… at first you make many lines, and then you only have to make a few, and they say more."

SELECTED BIBLIOGRAPHY

1. *Roger Hilton: Paintings and Drawings 1931 – 1973.*
Arts Council of Great Britain, London 1974.

2. *Roger Hilton: Night Letters and Selected Drawings.*
Newlyn Orion Galleries Limited, Newlyn 1980.

DAVID HOCKNEY b. 1937

David Hockney was born in Bradford, began his studies at the local art school and went on to the Royal College of Art where he studied from 1959 – 1962, graduating with the College's gold medal. His career was launched on the crest of the Pop Art wave and his work and personality attracted a degree of attention from the outset which has never significantly diminished. In 1963 a visit to Egypt laid the foundations of a recurrent interest in Egyptian art. During the next decade Hockney travelled extensively and his work reflected his appetite for new environments and his capacity for exploiting what he discovered. He lived in Paris in the early 1970s but has made California his home since then, although he retains an unabated enthusiasm for travel.

Hockney's work has moved through a wide range of styles and he has throughout his career been fascinated by techniques and materials. He has explored the potential of acrylic, oil, crayon, pastel, photography, stage design, moulded paper-pulp and every kind of graphic medium. He has however always held a brief for the 'subject' in his work, contrary to the fashions for 'abstraction' and 'expressionism' with which he grew up. Prints have been a major preoccupation all through his working life and he has won a number of international graphics prizes. In the 1980s Hockney built a new reputation for himself in the field of stage design.

His work has been exhibited in almost every country and major restrospectives have been held at the Whitechapel Art Gallery in 1970, in the Musée des Arts Décoratifs, Paris in 1974, the Tate Gallery in 1980 and the Los Angeles County Museum of Art in 1988.

SELECTED BIBLIOGRAPHY

1. *David Hockney by David Hockney.*
Thames and Hudson, London 1976.

2. *David Hockney* by Marco Livingstone.
Thames and Hudson, London 1981.

3. *David Hockney: A Retrospective.*
Los Angeles County Museum of Art, Los Angeles and Thames and Hudson, London 1988.

HOWARD HODGKIN b. 1932

Howard Hodgkin was born in London, the son of a prominent artistic family. After a year at Camberwell School of Art (1949) he studied at the Bath Academy of Art, from 1950 – 53, where he returned later as a teacher.

A personal style evolved slowly. Hodgkin's pictures of friends and places attempt to capture the abstract qualities of a particular time, place and area and to make permanent in pictorial form the impermanence of feeling. Close friends and passionate moments are the subjects of his work – painters he admires, the landscape of India he has come to know well or the particular flavour and after-taste of an affair.

In 1976 he was appointed Artist in Residence at Brasenose College, Oxford. The same year a retrospective of forty-five paintings was organised by the Arts Council. More recently, *Forty Paintings: 1973 – 84*, was shown as the British presentation at the Venice Biennale in 1984, and subsequently toured to America, Germany and Britain.

A prolific printmaker and noted collector of Indian paintings, Hodgkin has served as a Trustee of the Tate Gallery (1970 – 76) and the National Gallery, London (1978 – 85).

SELECTED BIBLIOGRAPHY

1. *Howard Hodgkin: Forty-Five Paintings 1949 – 75.*
Arts Council of Great Britain, London 1976.

2. *Howard Hodgkin: Forty Paintings 1973 – 84.*
The British Council, London 1984.

GWEN JOHN 1876 – 1939

Gwen John was born in Pembrokeshire, Wales, two years older than her brother, the painter Augustus John. After studying at the Slade School (1895 – 98), she briefly attended Whistler's Académie Cormon in Paris before deciding to settle in France permanently in 1904.

Throughout her career, John's subject matter was largely restricted to portraits of women and to interiors. She was received into the Roman Catholic Church in 1913. Her style changed little and was characterised by her simplicity of design and control of tone, mostly achieved in a limited range of low soft colours to produce a distinctive subtle lighting for her figures. The highly absorbent Japanese watercolour paper which she insisted on dictated a style of great control and economy. She produced numerous watercolours and drawings of the sisters and orphans of a neighbouring religious house as well as studies of cats and the room which she rarely left.

Her early years in Paris were supported by modelling for Rodin, and she moved to Meudon in 1911 close to Rodin's country house. Despite the patronage of an American collector, John Quinn, Gwen John led an increasingly penurious and solitary life, her last years spent as a virtual recluse.

SELECTED BIBLIOGRAPHY

1. *Gwen John: An Interior Life.*
Barbican Art Gallery, London 1985.

2. *Gwen John* by Cecily Langdale.
Yale University Press, London and New Haven 1987.

DAVID JONES 1895 – 1974

David Jones was a poet and novelist of distinction, as well as a painter. He was born in Kent of Welsh descent, and after military service during World War I studied at a London art school. He was converted to Catholicism in 1921, and throughout his life the symbols and liturgy of the church played an important part in his art. His novel, *In Parenthesis* (1937), about the experiences of the war and his poetry on the same subject brought him into prominence in the 1930s, but he suffered a nervous breakdown, and was thereafter dogged by mental illness. In 1932 he painted *Curtained Outlook* and the theme of looking out of one view onto another recurs frequently in his work, often as an indirect symbol of looking out of one world into another. In such scenes he included many of his primary interests – landscape, flowers and animals – all bound together in a delicate tracery of pencil or pen, and pale, transparent washes.

A major retrospective was held at the Tate Gallery in 1981.

SELECTED BIBLIOGRAPHY

1. *David Jones.*
Tate Gallery, London 1981.

2. *The Paintings of David Jones* by Nicolette Gray.
Lund Humphries, London 1989.

ANISH KAPOOR b. 1954

Anish Kapoor was born in Bombay, India. He spent two years in Israel (1971 – 73) before moving to Britain where he studied at Hornsey College of Art from 1973 – 77 and Chelsea School of Art from 1977 – 78. Artist-in-Residence at the Walker Art Gallery, Liverpool in 1982, he has since lived and worked in London.

A leading figure in the development of sculpture in Britain in the 1980s, Kapoor has steered a course which combines his cultural background with elements of Western modernism, in particular an interest in the work of Yves Klein and Joseph Beuys.

Although he has felt the influence of minimalism, Kapoor has never allowed its formalism to dominate his own more spiritual commitment to art. "I have no formal concerns; I don't wish to make sculpture about forms – it doesn't really interest me. I wish to make sculpture about belief, about passion, about experience, that is outside of material consideration."

Kapoor is a leading figure of the 'New British Sculpture' together with Tony Cragg (q.v.), Bill Woodrow (q.v.) and Richard Deacon (q.v.) and represented Britain at the Venice Biennale in 1990.

SELECTED BIBLIOGRAPHY

1. *Anish Kapoor On Paper 1975 – 1987.*
Ray Hughes Gallery, Queensland, Australia 1987.

2. *Anish Kapoor*
The British Council, London 1990.

PHILLIP KING b. 1934

Born in Kheredine, near Carthage in Tunisia, King came to England in 1946. He first began to make sculpture while reading modern languages at Cambridge University (1954 – 57). Immediately after he spent two years at St Martin's School of Art, largely because Anthony Caro (q.v.) was teaching there. In 1959 he began teaching at St Martin's himself and the same year worked as an assistant to Henry Moore (q.v.).

After travelling in Greece in 1960, King returned to London and started to make abstract sculpture. The use of fibreglass from 1962 allowed for a greater degree of experimentation, often on a large scale. Concentration, power and a certain élan are all characteristic of these big, abstract sculptures, which often contain elements of an Ozymandian grandeur. During this period he participated in several influential exhibitions, notably "The New Generation" (Whitechapel Art Gallery, London 1965) and "Primary Structures" (Jewish Museum, New York 1966). An important group of sculptures from the late 70s combined steel and wood in interlocking compositions.

King has received several important commissions, notably, a large steel sculpture, "Sky", for the Symposium for Sculptors organized for Expo '70 in Tokyo. During 1979 – 80 he was a Professor at the Hochschule der Kunste, West Berlin, and in 1980 he was appointed Professor of Sculpture at the Royal College of Art, London.

SELECTED BIBLIOGRAPHY

1. *Phillip King.*
Kröller-Muller National Museum, Otterlo 1974.

2. *Phillip King.*
Arts Council of Great Britain, London 1981.

R B KITAJ b. 1932

Born in Cleveland, Ohio, Kitaj's Jewish heritage and early migratory experiences of life were to have a significant bearing on his practice as an artist. He first studied art at the Cooper Union, New York, and after service with the US Army, took advantage of provisions in the GI Bill to settle in England to continue his art education.

As a mature student at the Royal College of Art his broad cultural interests in history, politics, literature and poetry were a significant influence on his fellow students, especially David Hockney (q.v.). Kitaj's preference for figuration provided a salutory alternative to the then prevailing influence of American abstraction. His ability to draw on a wide variety of historical and contemporary subjects and his adroit mix of drawing and painting, provided a model for a new form of picture-making.

In 1976 Kitaj conceived the influential exhibition, *The Human Clay*, which sought to reinstate the neglected values of figuration as a modern legacy; and he invented the term 'A School of London' to classify the group of painters, including Francis Bacon, Lucian Freud, (q.v.) Frank Auerbach (q.v.), and Leon Kossoff (q.v.) among others, who were all concerned with figurative painting as distinct from the fashionable international modernisms of the late 20th century.

In recent years, his work has shown increasing preoccupation with his own Jewish origins and the contemporary role of the Jewish people in the late twentieth century. He published 'A Diasporist Manifesto', a declaration of his views, in 1988.

A major retrospective exhibition was held in Washington, DC, Cleveland and Dusseldorf in 1981 – 82. He was elected to the Royal Academy in 1984 (the first American since Sargent).

SELECTED BIBLIOGRAPHY

1. *The Human Clay: An Exhibition Selected by R B Kitaj.*
Arts Council of Great Britain, London 1976.

2. *R B Kitaj.*
Hirshhorn Museum and Sculpture Garden, Smithsonian Institution, Washington DC 1981.

LEON KOSSOFF b. 1926

Leon Kossoff was born in London of Russian-Jewish parents. Since the age of twelve he has painted London obsessively:

"The strange, ever-changing lights, the endless streets, and the shuddering feel of the sprawling city linger in my mind like a faintly glimmering memory of a long-forgotten, perhaps never-experienced childhood."

Kossoff's paintings are characterised by rich surfaces of heavy impasto. Thick paint and sombre colours have recently given way to a lighter palette. His work has affinities with European expressionism, but also has particular English qualities, reminiscent of Sickert (q.v.) and the Camden Town Group of painters – an attachment to the everyday and least picturesque aspects of urban life.

From 1949 to 1953 Kossoff studied at the Borough Polytechnic, and attended David Bomberg's evening classes between 1950 and 1952. He studied painting at the Royal College of Art from 1953 – 56 and later taught at both Chelsea School of Art and the Regent Street Polytechnic. Kossoff's first one-man exhibition was at the Beaux Art Gallery in 1957. His most recent exhibition (shared with Bill Woodrow (q.v.)) was held at the Saatchi Collection, London, 1990.

SELECTED BIBLIOGRAPHY

1. *Leon Kossoff: Paintings From A Decade 1970 – 1980.*
Museum of Modern Art, Oxford 1981.

2. *Leon Kossoff.*
Anthony d'Offay Gallery, London 1988.

PETER LANYON b. 1918 – 64

The landscape of the Cornish coast surrounding St Ives, where Lanyon was born and spent much of his life, provided a constant source of inspiration for his painting thoughout his career.

Although he studied briefly at the Euston Road School, the more substantial influence on his work was provided by Ben Nicholson (q.v.) and the Russian constructivist sculptor, Naum Gabo, who settled in St Ives in 1939. Despite its geographical remoteness from London, St Ives, like Hampstead in the early 1930s, attracted several artists and intellectuals, and played an important role in influencing the course of British art.

Lanyon took as his subject the life, industry and landscape of the region – in particular the fishing and farming communities of south west Cornwall. The strong subject basis of his painting provided a foundation which he developed along increasingly abstract lines. During the 1950s his paintings became freer and more gestural, though the association with the landscape was never lost. Lanyon, and other St Ives' painters such as Roger Hilton (q.v.) were greatly encouraged by developments in American painting and friendships were forged with many leading American abstract expressionists.

Lanyon's passion for gliding, which he took up primarily to help him get to know the landscape better, provided him with new perspectives on the coast and shoreline which he integrated into his later paintings. Tragically, it also led to his death, caused by a gliding accident in 1964. Lanyon's work was the subject of a retrospective at the Tate Gallery in 1968.

SELECTED BIBLIOGRAPHY

1. *Peter Lanyon.*
Arts Council of Great Britain, London 1968.

2. *Peter Lanyon: Paintings, Drawings and Constructions 1937 – 64.*
Whitworth Art Gallery, University of Manchester 1978.

RICHARD LONG b. 1945

Richard Long was born in Bristol and continues to live in the area. A student at St Martin's School of Art from 1966 – 1968, Long and his contemporaries sought to challenge the prevailing concepts of sculpture. Whilst working within an English tradition of landscape art, Long's sympathy with the modern movements of Arte Povera and minimalism led to an extension of sculpture including the passage of time. This is most often expressed in his walks through uncluttered and remote landscapes. These sculptures are presented in the form of photographic, text or map works. Alternatively, the stones or pieces of wood which he finds on his walks are re-arranged in the gallery into floor sculptures, often in the form of simple, universal configurations, such as circles or lines.

Long's refined vocabulary of forms, classical restraint and sensitivity to place have considerably stretched the idea of what sculpture can be, frequently suggesting continuity with a past culture while remaining faithful to a limited range of simple, abstract means.

Since representing Britain at the Venice Biennale in 1976, he has had numerous acclaimed exhibitions, notably at the Guggenheim Museum, New York, in 1986.

A number of works in recent years have been made with mud from the local River Avon. Long has also produced a large number of books, mostly comprising photographic and textual works of art, recording his sculptures.

Long was awarded the Turner Prize in 1989.

SELECTED BIBLIOGRAPHY

1. *Richard Long.*
Van Abbemuseum, Eindhoven 1979.

2. *Richard Long.*
Solomon R. Guggenheim Museum, New York/Thames and Hudson, London 1986.

HENRY MOORE b. 1898 – 1986

Henry Moore was born in West Yorkshire in 1898, the seventh child of a mineworker, and studied at Leeds School of Art before going on to the Royal College of Art in 1921. A frequent visitor to the British Museum, he was greatly inspired by non-Western art, in particular the strong simplified forms of pre-Columbian Mexican art. Previously regarded in Britain solely as objects of archaeological or ethnographic interest, these were perceived by Moore as belonging to 'the mainstream of world sculpture'. His early work carved in stone displays his debt to his source in their simple monumentality and emphasis on their material qualities – 'stoniness' and sense of mass.

During the 1930s Moore's growing awareness of developments in modern art in France, and his interest in Picasso, encouraged a new morphological freedom in his sculpture. He participated in the International Surrealist Exhibition (1936) though remained at a distance from the extremes of both surrealism and abstraction. His own interests have always been rooted in the human form in its most elemental relationships, between mother and child, man and nature, and the forms in which these are cast: bone, rock, shell, skull, stone and hollow.

After the outbreak of World War II, Moore joined the War Artists' Scheme, achieving national recognition with his 'Shelter' drawings, inspired by London's underground stations where people took refuge from the Blitz.

Moore won the International Prize for Sculpture at the Venice Biennale in 1948. An established international reputation brought numerous commissions, and as a result he turned more and more to modelling and bronze casting. After the war, Moore lived in the country and continued to study and draw inspiration from natural objects.

SELECTED BIBLIOGRAPHY

1. *The Life of Henry Moore* by Roger Berthoud. Faber and Faber, London 1987.

2. *Henry Moore.*
Royal Academy of Arts, London 1988.

3. *Henry Moore: Sculpture and Drawings* (5 vols). ed. Alan Bowness. Lund Humphries, London 1944 – 1983

PAUL NASH 1889 – 1946

Born in London, Paul Nash originally intended to join the navy, but after failing his naval entrance, took evening art classes and entered the Slade School in 1910. He was appointed an Official War Artist in 1917. Between the wars he designed textiles, stage scenery, costumes and ceramics, as well as painting in oil and watercolour. All of his work shows a characteristically analytical approach, reducing a subject to its essential form, but remaining conscious of the irreducible mystery in all matter. His touch is typically gentle and delicate; none of his forms, however abstract, are made to look entirely mechanical or geometric. During the 1930s he was fascinated by surrealism, by the power of objects to evoke associations alien to their basic forms, and his own work reveals these preoccupations. Objects which held special meaning for him – the sun and moon, the sunflower and fungus, early burial relics, rocks, the sea and clumps of trees – are drawn together in landscapes empty of people, but which suggest their presence. In 1933 he established Unit One, a group of artists that included Henry Moore (q.v.), Wadsworth (q.v.), Burra (q.v.) and Nicholson (q.v.) and whose aims were to promote modern art through a blend of abstraction and surrealism. During World War II he was again appointed an Official War Artist, producing memorable images of the war-torn countryside which in turn are sinister and lyrical, surreal yet rooted in the traditions of English landscape painting.

SELECTED BIBLIOGRAPHY

1. *Paul Nash* by Andrew Causey. Clarendon Press, Oxford 1980.

2. *Outline: An Autobiography* by Paul Nash. Faber and Faber, London 1951.

BEN NICHOLSON 1894 – 1982

Nicholson is one of the most influential British artists of this century, celebrated for his ability to synthesise and abstract from nature its bare essentials and re-form them in compositions of extreme elegance and clarity. He was born in Buckinghamshire, the son of a landscape painter, and apart from one term spent at the Slade School, had no formal art education. He was a member of Unit One (see Paul Nash) from 1933. He spent some time travelling abroad before settling in London between 1932 – 39, but it was on his move to the small fishing town of St Ives on the coast of Cornwall that his art took new directions. For the most part his paintings and reliefs are geometrically organised, playing formal and austere lines against blocks of subdued colour, achieving a balance between line and suggested volume. He always retained his interest in landscape, and the clear, bright light of Cornwall was probably instrumental in developing his sense of light, almost transparent colour, through which objects are filtered rather than merely described.

SELECTED BIBLIOGRAPHY

1. *Ben Nicholson.*
Tate Gallery, London 1969.

2. *Ben Nicholson: The Years of Experiments 1919 – 39.*
Kettle's Yard Gallery, University of Cambridge 1983.

EDUARDO PAOLOZZI b. 1924

Paolozzi was brought up in Edinburgh, of Italian parentage, and first studied at the city's College of Art, then at the Slade School in Oxford and London.

A period of two years in Paris (1947 – 49) brought him into direct contact with new ideas in art, particularly with primitive art at the Musée de l'Homme. Under the influence of Dada and surrealism, Paolozzi began to develop his distinctive collagist approach to handling material.

Paolozzi's interest in the mass media and in new developments in science and technology was formalised in the foundation of The Independent Group in 1952, a like-minded group of artists, theorists, architects and critics. Based at the Institute of Contemporary Art, London, the group set a new programme of aesthetics attacking the cosiness of postwar British culture, and promoting the urban over the pastoral, the public over the private mode of expression, the embrace of 'commercialisation' and mass marketing.

Paolozzi's sculpture at the time was often influenced by industrial techniques, mostly executed in aluminium and either brightly polished or painted. Contemporaneously, he produced three important series of collage-based prints.

Commissioned by London Underground to decorate Tottenham Court Road station in 1979, other public commissions have followed in both Britain and Germany. Lecturer in ceramics at the Royal College of Art since 1968, he was appointed Professor of Sculpture at the Akademie der Bildenden Kunste, Munich, in 1981. Paolozzi's eclecticism, his favoured 'borrowings' and 'raidings' from various cultural cupboards, were exemplified in the exhibition he produced for the Museum of Mankind, *Lost Magic Kingdoms*, 1985.

SELECTED BIBLIOGRAPHY

1. *Eduardo Paolozzi Sculpture, Drawings, Collages and Graphics.*
Arts Council of Great Britain, London 1976.

2. *Eduardo Paolozzi: Lost Magic Kingdoms.*
British Museum, London 1985.

ERIC RAVILIOUS 1903 – 1942

Born in London, Ravilious studied first at Eastbourne, then at the Royal College of Art. His talents for design were many: he produced woodcarvings for book illustration, designed pottery and engraved glass, and through each of these media he insinuated a wry innocence, a sense of slight strangeness that characterises all his work. In his watercolours, he brought his 'innocent eye' to English rural subjects, bending the rules so to speak to produce delicate fantasies out of well-known entities such as greenhouses and watering cans. At the outbreak of war in 1939, he was appointed an Official War Artist, and produced an outstanding body of work from then until his death three years later in an air-crash over Iceland. The bizarre quality of war is made to look almost normal in Ravilious' strange juxtapositions of rainbows and mooring posts, dazzle-camouflage and piebald skies, coastal defences and stars that appear to shoot from the ground rather than from the sky (searchlights).

SELECTED BIBLIOGRAPHY

1. *The England of Eric Ravilious* by Freda Constable. Scolar Press, London 1982.

2. *Eric Ravilious: Memoir of an Artist* by Helen Binyon. Lutterworth Press, Guildford and London 1983.

BRIDGET RILEY b. 1931

Born in London, Riley spent the war years in Cornwall. After a spasmodic start to her education. she returned to London to study at Goldsmiths' College of Art from 1949 – 52, graduating to the Royal College of Art in 1952.

Riley's approach to painting was slow to evolve and it was not until 1960 that she made her first essays in optical painting during visits to Spain and Italy. All her paintings of the early 1960s were in black and white. Riley quickly developed a style comprising regular patterns of line and colour which cover the entire surface of the painting and appear to shift and vibrate while they are in fact static and rigid. Colour was introduced in 1966, first as warmer and cooler greys, than as vivid contrasting pairs such as red and turquoise. She described these works thus: 'They are concerned with principles of repose and disturbance... in each of them a particular situation is stated visually. Certain elements within that situation remain constant. Others precipitated the destruction of themselves by themselves. Recurrently, as a result of the cyclic movement of repose, disturbance, and repose, the original situation was restated'.

Riley won the International Prize for Painting at the 34th Venice Biennale 1968 and the following year established SPACE, a scheme for organising artists' studios.

SELECTED BIBLIOGRAPHY

1. *Bridget Riley: Paintings and Drawings 1951 – 71.*
Arts Council of Great Britain, London 1971.

2. *Bridget Riley: Works 1959-78.*
British Council, London 1978.

WILLIAM ROBERTS 1895 – 1950

The son of a London carpenter, Roberts started work at the age of fourteen in the office of an advertising agency, but won a scholarship to the Slade School in 1910. There he was influenced by Cubism, and soon after leaving the Slade, was producing work with an emphasis on simplification, flat pattern and strong outline. For a time he worked with one of England's most influential critics of modern art, Roger Fry, painting fabrics and furniture with Cubist designs. He then joined a group of artists called The Rebel Art Centre, whose beliefs centred on the necessity of making art reflect the mechanical qualities of modern life. The main features of Roberts' art were already set by this date, and were not to alter substantially for the rest of his life. Tubular limbed figures are shown in group activities, often emphasising their mechanical qualities, usually brightly coloured and with a strong sense of rhythm: they approximate to a sort of flexible geometry.

SELECTED BIBLIOGRAPHY

1. *William Roberts ARA: Retrospective Exhibition.*
Arts Council of Great Britain, London 1965.

2. *William Roberts 1895 – 1980: An Artist and his Family.*
National Portrait Gallery, London 1984.

SEAN SCULLY b. 1945

Born in Dublin, Scully's family moved to London in 1949. He studied first at Croydon College of Art, then Newcastle University until 1972, when a fellowship took him to Harvard University. In 1975 he moved to the USA and has since lived and worked in New York, spending summers in London.

Scully's paintings of the early 1970's were characterised by a grid structure. Soaked and sprayed acrylic on canvas were to be replaced by hand-brushed oil paints (1976 – 80) and horizontal patterns of stripes. Scully has maintained an unfailing commitment to a position now considered unfashionable in many quarters.

Scully received a Guggenheim Fellowship in 1983, the year he became an American citizen. A survey exhibition organised by the Whitechapel Art Gallery, 1989, was shown in London, Munich and Madrid.

SELECTED BIBLIOGRAPHY

1. *Sean Scully.*
Carnegie Institute, Pittsburgh 1985.

2. *Sean Scully: Paintings and Works on Paper 1982 – 1988.*
Whitechapel Art Gallery, London 1989.

WALTER RICHARD SICKERT 1860 – 1942

Born in Germany to an Anglo-Irish mother and a Danish father, Sickert's family moved to England in 1868. An intended career in the theatre lasted four years but was abandoned in favour of painting and he entered the Slade School in 1881.

As a pupil and assistant to Whistler he learnt the art of etching, as well as a subtle tonal approach to painting that he was to draw on throughout his life. The influence of Degas, whom he met in 1883 was greater, bringing him into contact with the modern movement in France and forcing him to see the restrictions of contemporary art in England.

From the late 1880s he regularly visited Dieppe, and later Venice, where architectural views formed his principal subject. In England, he was drawn to theatres and vaudeville, which combined his love of drama with a feeling for the tawdriness of urban interiors.

An outspoken and forceful protagonist for painting, Sickert became the leader of a group of urban realist painters who gathered in his studio in Fitzroy Street, the nucleus of which was to become the Camden Town Group, named after the district of London in which he lived. They became renowned for their depiction of the seedy London world of this run-down area. Female nudes, couples in bedrooms and domestic scenes in front parlours dominate Sickert's painting at this period, giving, in his words, 'the sensation of a page torn from the Book of Life'.

An important teacher, both Sickert's early and late work – the latter based on photography and newspapers – have influenced successive generations of painters – most particularly the artists grouped as a 'School of London' – (see R B Kitaj).

SELECTED BIBLIOGRAPHY

1. *Walter Richard Sickert,* by Wendy Baron. Phaidon Press Limited, London 1973.

2. *Paintings, Drawings and Prints of Walter Richard Sickert 1860 – 1942.* Arts Council of Great Britain, London 1977.

MATTHEW SMITH 1879 – 1959

Born in Halifax, Smith rebelled against his family's insistence that he join the family manufacturing business. He studied art instead, first at the Manchester School of Technology, then at the Slade School in London from 1905 – 8.

Visits to France encouraged his interest in French painting, but the outbreak of war found him in England. He took a studio in Fitzroy Street in 1916, where Sickert (q.v.) was his neighbour.

A gifted and sensual colourist, Smith was equally attracted to the work of the Old Masters, as he was to Gauguin and the French Fauve painters. Despite living for extended periods in Paris, his early work, especially the Fitzroy Street nudes and Cornish landscapes, belong to the development of Post-Impressionism in Britain. These works possess a muscular vigour and directness quite alien to the predominant styles of painting in Britain at the time and are still remarkable for their immediacy.

During World War II both Smith's sons were killed and, separated from his wife, he lived an increasingly solitary existence. He was knighted in 1954.

A large group of his paintings were shown at the Venice Biennale of 1950 and a retrospective held at the Tate Gallery in 1953, and at the Barbican Art Gallery in 1983.

SELECTED BIBLIOGRAPHY

1. *Matthew Smith 1879 – 1959: Paintings from the Artists Studio.* Arts Council of Great Britain, London 1972.

2. *Matthew Smith.* Barbican Art Gallery, London 1983.

RICHARD SMITH b. 1931

Born in Hertfordshire, Smith studied at the Royal College of Art and saw military service with the RAF in Hong Kong from 1950 – 52. He spent several years painting and teaching in America, and much of his early work was concerned with the imagery and ideas of American culture – packaging, in particular. He was never, however, interested in simply painting replicas of the objects he found interesting, but rather in trying to find ways of representing them in a two-dimensional form. His work gradually became more minimal, often painted in one colour with a second colour used only as an accent. In trying to find ways of transposing ideas, Smith began to question the two-dimensional properties of art itself, as well as the conventional materials of painting in the west – canvas and stretcher – and to find new ways by which a painting could express the shape of reality as he saw it. He began to take the canvas off the stretcher, letting it hang loose, or tied with knots, to suggest sails or kites – objects which could change with new directions rather than being held rigid against a wall, and taking painting close to the realm of sculpture.

SELECTED BIBLIOGRAPHY

1. *Richard Smith: Paintings 1958 – 1966.* Whitechapel Art Gallery, London 1966.

2. *Richard Smith: Seven Exhibitions 1961 – 1975.* Tate Gallery, London 1975.

STANLEY SPENCER 1891 – 1959

One of the most original painters of this century, Spencer was born in the Thameside village of Cookham, where his father was a music teacher and church organist. As a child, Spencer's remarkable visual imagination helped him to visualise Cookham as the centre of historical and religious events, so that when he read about such miraculous events as the Resurrection of the Dead he imagined them happening locally, to the butcher, the baker, the local postman and the village schoolmaster. He studied at the Slade School from 1908 – 1912 and saw active service during World War II. His war experiences became the subject of his first important commission. During World War II, he was appointed an Official War Artist, and commissioned to paint the shipbuilding yards on the Clyde. He belonged to no school or movement, although it would be true to say that he is an essentially English artist: obsessive about detail, about portraying local events, about the countryside in which he grew up, and none too bothered about the fashions and developments in art abroad. He was knighted in 1958.

SELECTED BIBLIOGRAPHY

1. *Stanley Spencer: A biography* by Maurice Collis. Harvill Press, London 1962.

2 *Stanley Spencer at War* by Richard Carline. Faber and Faber, London 1978.

3. *Stanley Spencer RA.* Royal Academy of Arts, London 1980.

GRAHAM SUTHERLAND 1903 – 79

Born in London, Sutherland worked as an apprentice at a locomotive works before starting his training at a London art school. From 1928 – 32 he taught etching, engraving and book illustration. His real development as a painter dates from 1935, when he visited Pembrokeshire in the Welsh border country, and began a series of paintings based on landscape and natural forms. In 'moments of vision' he felt that things were taking on a life of their own, and undergoing a metamorphis from a static, fixed shape, to an undefined, indeterminate form. In his own words, he was fascinated by the 'whole problem of the tensions produced by the power of growth'. He was appointed an Official War Artist in 1940. The subjects roused by the war – armaments factories, shattered masonry, the twisted iron of blitzed cities – all confirmed Sutherland in his instinct of a cruel, unapprehending world, and he chose a palette of intense, cold colours to reinforce this impression. After the war, he concentrated on images which made this impression even more forceful, in particular the thorn tree, an obsessive symbol of cruelty. From the mid '50s he spent at least half of every year in France, increasingly establishing a reputation as a portrait, as well as a landscape, painter.

SELECTED BIBLIOGRAPHY

1. *Graham Sutherland,* Tate Gallery, London 1982.

2. *Graham Sutherland: Correspondences,* edited by Julian Andrews. The Graham and Kathleen Sutherland Foundation, Haverfordwest 1982.

JOHN TUNNARD 1900 – 1971

Born in Bedfordshire, Tunnard studied textile design at the Royal College of Art from 1919 – 1923, and subsequently worked as a designer in a carpet factory for a period of ten years. He was also a keen jazz player. At the beginning of the 1930s he and his wife moved to Cornwall and established a hand-block printed silk business, and Tunnard began to devote himself increasingly to painting. Much of the imagery he used derives from the seashore where he lived and worked, though some seem to come from the idiom of jazz: his weird, impromptu shapes, cut with a metallic edge, often seem to be the visual metaphors for this modern, free-association music. He always maintained an interest in natural history, and his attention to animal and plant life is also apparent in much of his work. In addition he was a keen field botanist, and collected rare insects for the British Museum.

SELECTED BIBLIOGRAPHY

1. *John Tunnard,* by Denys Sutton. McRoberts and Tunnard London 1959.

2. *John Tunnard 1900 – 1971.* Arts Council of Great Britain, London 1977.

EDWARD WADSWORTH 1889 – 1949

Wadsworth was born in Yorkshire, the son of a wealthy manufacturer. At the age of sixteen he went to Germany to study engineering and in his spare time studied at an art school. He returned to England to attend a local art school in the north of England, and in 1910 won a scholarship to the Slade School. Before the war he was attracted by the ideals of the Vorticists, an avant-garde group whose aim was to reflect the mechanical and technological advances that were rapidly affecting the face of 20th century society – as a result, much of their work looks consciously abstract and mechanistic. During World War II, Wadsworth served with the navy and was one of the first artists to adapt military inventions such as 'dazzle-camouflage' to the formal patterns of his art. His work of this period, including the drawing *Ladle Slag*, concentrated on taking unpicturesque subject matter (Ladle Slag was a field of waste products from the industrial midlands of the country, so-called because of the ladles used to scoop up the refuse and dump it on a heap) and transforming it into an image of inherent strength and energy. After the war he concentrated largely on wood engraving and drawing. He became increasingly drawn to nautical subjects, and his later work has a typically surreal quality, often displaying odd assortments of objects thrown together with no obvious connection, and yet drawn with a meticulous, precision-cut clarity.

SELECTED BIBLIOGRAPHY

1. *Edward Wadsworth 1889 – 1949: Paintings, Drawings and Prints.*
P & D Colnaghi, London 1974.

2. *Edward Wadsworth: A Painter's Life,* by Barbara Wadsworth. Michael Russell Ltd, Salisbury 1989

BOYD WEBB b. 1947

Boyd Webb was born in Christchurch, New Zealand, and later settled in London, studying sculpture at the Royal College of Art from 1972 to 1975. He began to make life-casts of people in fibreglass arranged in tableaux, but soon rejected the practice as costly and cumbersome, and took to photography.

"I use photography because it is an essential fact of the age and I believe an artist should use the materials and techniques of his time. Photography is a flexible medium, capable of being stretched in many directions. Tolerant of much abuse it always retains an inherent honesty – it can reproduce with great clarity even the most featureless of man-made materials."

Webb's subversive play on the 'inherent honesty' of the medium provides the tension between the real and the imagined in his deceptive and theatrical photographic tableaux.

Webb's early photographs portray figures acting out bizarre and surreal actions. More mysterious and elaborate compositions followed, created from constructed sets built by the artist in his studio. In his more recent work, an underlying concern for man's relationship with nature surfaces in depictions of inflatable toy animals, often set against backgrounds of garish, unnatural colour. The allegorical implication that humanity's disregard for the planet may lead to nature's final revenge is conveyed with Webb's characteristic irony, and melancholic humour.

SELECTED BIBLIOGRAPHY

1. *Boyd Webb.*
Whitechapel Art Gallery, London 1978.

2. *Boyd Webb.*
Stedelijk Van Abbemuseum, Eindhoven 1983.

BILL WOODROW b. 1948

Born near Henley, Oxfordshire, Woodrow studied at St. Martin's School of Art from 1968 – 71 and Chelsea School of Art from 1971 – 72. He began to develop an approach to sculpture, which, in common with his contemporary Tony Cragg (q.v.), recognised the conflicts between modern society's aspirations and their impact on the world.

His early sculptures were made from everyday objects such as bicycles and hoovers, which were first embedded in plaster or concrete and then partially excavated, like fossils or archaeological remains, until their identities re-emerged. They combine a fascination with material goods and a comment on the culture that gives them birth, a combination that has become a hallmark of his work.

By the early 1980s he had developed a technique in which a sculpture was constructed or "re-cycled" from the metal sheeting or skin of a discarded consumer object like a washing machine or a car part. The various elements of the sculpture, physically linked by the umbilical metal, combined to create a new image. The social commentary implicit in Woodrow's work combines humour and gravitatas in equal measure.

A major survey of his work was held at the Fruitmarket Gallery, Edinburgh, in 1986 and he has participated in numerous exhibitions of contemporary British sculpture. An invitation to exhibit new work at the Imperial War Museum in 1990 led to his first sculptures in bronze.

SELECTED BIBLIOGRAPHY

1. *Beaver, Bomb and Fossil.*
Museum of Modern Art, Oxford 1983.

2. *Bill Woodrow: Sculpture 1980 – 1986.*
Fruitmarket Gallery, Edinburgh 1986.